MAKING
polymer
clay
beads

Step-by-step techniques for creating
beautiful ornamental beads

MAKING
polymer
clay
beads

Step-by-step techniques for creating
beautiful ornamental beads

Carol Blackburn

INTERWEAVE PRESS
interweavebooks.com

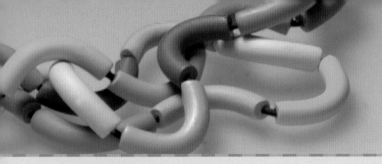

A QUARTO BOOK
Copyright © 2007 Quarto Inc.

INTERWEAVE PRESS
interweavebooks.com
Published in North America by
Interweave Press LLC
201 East Fourth Street
Loveland, CO 80537-5655, USA

Library of Congress Cataloging-in-Publication Data

Blackburn, Carol, 1946-
  Making polymer clay beads: step-by-step techniques for creating beautiful ornamental beads / Carol Blackburn, author.
      p. cm.
  Includes index.
  ISBN-13: 978-1-59668-019-7 (pbk.)
  1. Polymer clay craft. 2. Beads. I. Title.

TT297.B54 2007
745.58'2--dc22

2006032125

Conceived, designed, and produced by
Quarto Publishing plc
The Old Brewery
6 Blundell Street
London N7 9BH

SENIOR EDITORS Liz Dalby, Jo Fisher
DESIGNERS Louise Clements, Michelle Stamp
DESIGN ASSISTANT Jess Wilson
COPY EDITOR Claire Wedderburn-Maxwell
PROOFREADER Noo Saro-Wiwa
PHOTOGRAPHER Paul Forrester
INDEXER Diana LeCore

ART DIRECTOR Moira Clinch
PUBLISHER Paul Carslake

MANUFACTURED BY Modern Age Repro House Ltd, Hong Kong
PRINTED BY SNP Leefung, China

QUAR.PCBM
10 9 8 7 6 5 4 3

CONTENTS

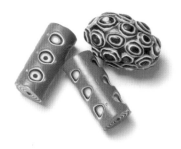

FOREWORD

While visiting a bead fair looking for interesting buttons and beads for my knitwear, I stumbled across the British Polymer Clay Guild stand and was awestruck by the clay techniques being demonstrated by guild members. I bought a necklace (see Gallery page 121), and booked a class. I was hooked.

Since then—although I still have a passion for tassels and braids— polymer clay has occupied all of my free time at the expense of my textiles work. I discovered that the polymer clay world, both online and in reality, is friendly and sharing and as a result I've made many friends in both North America and Europe, without whose encouragement and enthusiasm this book might never have happened.

I use a ringbinder for keeping a record of color mixtures and baking times.

The basics of polymer clay are quickly mastered even if you are new to the material. After trying a few step-by-step projects based on the key techniques and basic bead shapes, you should be able to begin experimenting with your own bead designs and some of the more ambitious faux projects. The gallery chapter of the book is designed to inspire and show what can be achieved in terms of design as well as technique.

MATERIALS & TECHNIQUES

From basic information on working with polymer clay to more unusual and exciting effects, all with clear, step-by-step instructions.

Tools & Materials

Gallery strip showing finished beads and possible variations

Numbered step-by-step instructions with clear, detailed photographs

Cross sections and bead details for extra clarity

FAUX EFFECTS

Techniques for making exquisite beads that mimic natural materials, from metals to semiprecious stones, ivory and coral, and leather.

More ideas for the application of the technique

"See also" tells you where to look for related articles

GALLERY

An inspirational selection of work by leading polymer clay artists.

TECHNIQUES

MATERIALS

POLYMER CLAY IS A VERSATILE synthetic modeling material that is soft and malleable until it is baked, when it becomes hard. It consists of pigments and PVC particles, bound together by a plasticizer. It is available in a wide range of colors that can be mixed together to produce an even wider color palette. Other materials such as paints and powders can be used with polymer clay and are useful as part of your basic toolkit.

POLYMER CLAY BRANDS

Brands vary slightly in stiffness and strength before and after baking. Try them out to find what suits you. The main brands are Fimo, Premo! Sculpey, and Kato.

Fimo is made in two forms: Fimo Classic, a firm clay, which is difficult to condition; and Fimo Soft, which is easier to condition. Try mixing equal amounts of both clays to produce a medium-firm consistency. Many polymer clay artists use Fimo as it holds fine detail well during cane reduction.

Premo! Sculpey is easy to condition but can become too soft if it is handled a lot or your hands are hot. However, it will firm up if left to cool before slicing. Fimo and Premo! are sold in 2 oz (56 g) blocks or blocks of 1 lb (450 g), and both types of clay sand and buff well after baking. **Kato** is a promising new high-quality product that is available in 3 oz (85 g) blocks.

Most of the beads in this book are made with Fimo (classic and soft) and Premo!, and the two are often mixed together to create a particular color or a more workable consistency, although this is not always recommended by manufacturers. Each manufacturer makes twenty to thirty solid colors of polymer clay as well as various specialty clays that can be mixed with solid colors or used on their own.

MICA CLAYS

Mica clays have tiny particles of pearl, gold, silver, or copper. After conditioning with a pasta machine, the mica particles align. You can create shimmering effects by cutting and rearranging the clay.

BAKE AND BEND

Sculpey Bake and Bend clay is rubbery and flexible after baking. It can be extruded (see page 50) and made into braid, or used for a cord, as in the Cinnabar pendants (see page 36).

SCULPEY ULTRA LIGHT

Sculpey Ultra Light is ideal as a low-weight bead core for large beads. The Ultra Light clay bead on the right weighs the same as the smaller Fimo clay bead on the left.

METALLIC POWDERS

Metallic powders are available in many different colors. They can be applied with a soft brush or fingertip to raw clay.

When baked they produce a metallic or iridescent effect. They can also be mixed into varnish or liquid clay.

► **Tip**
► Store new blocks of clay in a cool place away from sunlight. Once opened, raw clay should be kept covered to prevent dust or hair sticking to it. Use partitioned, lidded metal or polythene boxes.

ADHESIVES

Liquid or gel superglues provide a strong bond. They set immediately and are useful for joining baked clay to metal findings or rubber cord.

Two-part epoxy glues are good for joining baked clays together or attaching metal findings to baked clay.

Unbaked clay usually sticks to baked clay, but priming with liquid polymer clay ensures they bond during rebaking.

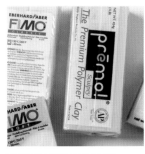

TRANSLUCENT CLAY

Translucent clay is colorless and can be used on its own or mixed with colored clay. During baking, it may "plaque," producing disks in the clay. This can be useful for faux techniques such as Jade (see page 86). Translucent clay with bleach, such as Premo Frost, is less likely to plaque.

EMBOSSING POWDERS

Embossing powders expand when heated. They are often sprinkled on to wet ink-patterns that have been applied with rubber stamps. They stick to raw polymer clay and can be mixed into it for textured effects.

LIQUID CLAY

This viscous clay can be used as a softener or to bond baked and unbaked clay. It can be tinted with oil paint to make an enamel or mixed with glitters and powders for decorative effects.

SCRAP CLAY

Scrap clay is extremely useful. Keep it in airtight boxes. It can be used for bead cores (where it is covered), for casting molds, for backing a decorative sheet, or with metallic powders.

CLAY SOFTENERS

Sculpey Diluent clay softener or Fimo Mix Quick can be used to soften hardened clay. Always follow the manufacturer's instructions when using these products.

PAINTS

Acrylic paints are the best paints to use on polymer clay—do not use enamel paints. Water-based acrylic paint is waterproof once dry and can be used for creating a patina effect on beads.

Artists' oil paint can be used sparingly, mixed into clay or liquid polymer clay, or used for feathering effects. It is also used for the Faux Abalone beads (see page 84).

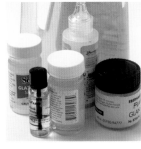

VARNISHES

Use water-based acrylic varnishes, such as Future, rather than solvent-based varnishes, which may never dry or remain sticky. Ranger's Poly-Glaze is water-soluble and is useful for building up a thick, glass-like finish. It must be varnished to make it waterproof.

Manufacturers also make varnishes for polymer clay. Most are water-based and come in gloss, matt, or satin.

INCLUSIONS

You can mix anything that can withstand baking into polymer clay, including metallic and iridescent powders, metal leaf and foils, glitter and embossing powders, sand, dried aromatic herbs and spices, and seeds. It is preferable to add inclusions to translucent clays where they are revealed to best effect.

RELEASE AGENTS

Polymer clay takes the impression of whatever it is pressed against, so some very decorative surface textures and molded shapes can be incorporated into beads. However, the clay tends to stick unless a release agent is used. Water, cornstarch, talcum powder, and Armor All spray are all used to prevent stamps, molds, and texture sheets from sticking.

HEALTH AND SAFETY

Polymer clay is nontoxic, but if you have sensitive skin or are handling polymer clay for many hours at a time, consider wearing surgical gloves.

Polymer clay can give off noxious fumes if it is baked at a higher-than-recommended temperature. Bake it in a well-ventilated room and if the oven does overheat, open the windows and leave the room until the fumes have disappeared. Never use a microwave oven to bake polymer clay.

Wear a dust mask when using metallic or any fine powders.

EQUIPMENT AND WORKSPACE

YOU WILL PROBABLY ALREADY HAVE the basic equipment you need to begin working with polymer clay at home. To start, you will only require a smooth and shiny work surface, a sharp knife, a rolling pin, a piercing tool, and an oven to bake your beads in. As you work with polymer clay and start to make more varied projects, gradually add tools to your collection.

Although polymer clays are nontoxic, do not use the same tools for clay that you use for food preparation. Use hand wipes rather than soap for cleaning your hands, work surfaces, and tools.

WORK SURFACE
You will need a smooth and shiny work surface, such as a ¼" (6 mm) thick sheet of glass with sanded edges, or a smooth tile. A slab of marble also makes a smooth surface that will help keep clay cool in hot weather. Formica or melamine boards also make excellent work surfaces.

CRAFT KNIFE
A craft knife with a straight or a curved blade is useful for cutting logs, trimming clay, or picking up small pieces of clay and applying them to a bead, as in Appliqué beads (see page 54).

TISSUE BLADES
Tissue blades are straight, stainless steel blades, 4–6" (100–150 mm) long. They are extremely sharp, so mark the blunt edge with a dot of colored nail polish to avoid picking up the wrong edge. They are flexible, and as well as making straight cuts can be used to cut curved shapes or to remove a mark from a rolled sheet of clay.

Save the pieces cut with a ripple blade from the sides of a layered jelly roll to use as onlays on an oval bead.

RIPPLE BLADES
Ripple blades have a wavy cutting edge and are useful for generating new and interesting shapes and patterns, such as Jigsaw beads (see page 29), Ripple beads (see page 67), and Mokume Gane beads (see page 62).

ROLLING SLICER
A rolling slicer has a row of circular cutters that roll and cut the clay sheet into several strips at the same time. A rolling slicer is excellent for cutting a thin sheet into small square tiles for mosaics and onlays.

COOKIE CUTTERS
Confectionery and catering departments of stores are a good source for miniature cookie cutters and molds in a wide variety of styles.

LINOLEUM CUTTERS
A linoleum cutter is useful for carving divots and grooves from a clay block or sheet, as in the Appliqué beads (see page 54).

▶ **Tip**
▶ Use a piece of plain paper as a disposable cutting board. The clay is easily turned for cutting from different angles and distorts less when peeled away from the paper. It also saves the knife blade from blunting against a tile or glass work surface.

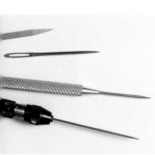

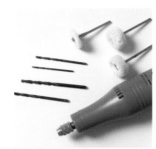

PIERCING TOOLS

You will need a collection of different piercing tools for making a variety of holes in unbaked beads.

ELECTRIC CRAFT TOOL

An electric craft tool can be used for drilling holes in baked clay and for polishing using a cotton mop-head attachment, or an unstitched muslin, mounted wheel that fits the craft tool's collet.

DRILL AND DRILL BITS

A drill and drill bits of various sizes are useful for enlarging holes in baked beads. Use a reamer or a needle file to enlarge small holes.

BALL STYLUSES

Ball styluses come in several different sizes and are used for making holes in clay stacks, as in Faux Abalone (see page 84).

FOOD PROCESSOR

Useful but not essential, a food processor is a great way to chop up stiff clay. As it warms and softens the clay at the same time, use the processor in short bursts to prevent the clay from clumping and causing damage. A food processor is good for mixing colors but the mix will need finishing by hand or with a pasta machine.

HAND GRATERS

Hand graters do the same job as food processors but more slowly. Use a mini-grater for grating baked clay into tiny bits for using as inclusions, as in the Faux Jade beads (see page 86).

TEXTURING TOOLS

Texture contributes to the character of beads as much as shape, pattern, and color. There is a wide range of texture sheets and rubber stamps available, as well as objects around the home that can be used (see also page 55). Flexible texture sheets and leaves can be impressed into the clay or rolled through a pasta machine with the clay. Use a release agent such as water or cornstarch (see page 11) when using textured sheets or objects.

The sheet below has been textured simply, using pen-tops to create a variety of round and star-shaped indentations in the clay.

PAINTBRUSHES

You will need various sizes of paintbrushes for applying paints or metallic powders, for antiquing, painting, glazing with liquid clays, and varnishing. Paintbrush handles can also be useful for supporting beads while you decorate them.

EXTRUDER TOOLS

Several brands of extruder tools are available. The barrel of the extruder is loaded with clay. A plunger is inserted and pressed against the clay so the clay is forced out through a shaped die. An adapter makes extruding clay even easier as extra pressure can be applied to the extruder.

Alternatively, a garlic press can be used to extrude small lengths of clay.

If a small extruder is difficult to clean, heat it for a few minutes in a hot oven to harden the clay residue, which can then be chipped or peeled off.

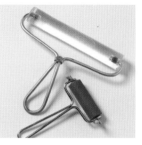

PASTA MACHINE

Pasta machines are almost indispensable when working with polymer clay. They are made by several different manufacturers and have settings ranging from thick to thin. It is quick and easy to condition clay, roll sheets of various thicknesses and make Skinner blends with a pasta machine. You can also fit an electric motor to the machine, thus freeing both hands to hold long, thin sheets of clay as they are rolled through.

Always follow the manufacturer's instructions and avoid damaging the spacing of the rollers by not forcing too thick a slice of clay between them.

ROLLING TOOLS

Most rolling of clay sheets is best done with a pasta machine, but sometimes stacks of thin sheets have to be consolidated or a sheet is needed that is thicker than the machine can handle. To roll very thick sheets of clay, use two identical knitting needles, pencils, or pieces of wood, and place them on either side of the clay. Roll the roller over them and they will help maintain an even thickness (see page 18). Use a similar arrangement with a glass sheet with sanded edges to roll "logs". A clear acrylic roller allows you to see what is happening to the clay as you roll.

BRAYER

A brayer is a roller with a handle, which allows you to roll with one hand and hold the clay with the other. A narrow brayer is useful for reshaping a cane into a triangular or square cane. Brayers can be made of rubber or clear acrylic. Use a brayer for controlled "crazing" of metal foil on a clay sheet (see page 52).

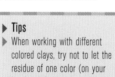

▶ **Tips**

▶ When working with different colored clays, try not to let the residue of one color (on your hands or the pasta machine) spoil the next color you work with. Work with the lightest color first, then progress to the darker colors. Wipe the pasta machine clean with paper towels, a soft cloth, or hand wipes between colors.

▶ For ultrathin sheets of clay, that are thinner than the thinnest setting on your pasta machine, place the already-rolled thin clay between two sheets of wax paper, then run through the pasta machine.

OVEN

Ideally, you should have a portable worktop oven just for polymer clay; a fan convection oven bakes the clay more evenly. You can use a domestic oven, but use a lidded casserole dish or make a "tent" out of paper or aluminum foil to contain any plasticizer that is volatilized by the heat. Do not use a microwave oven; overheating can cause polymer clay to give off noxious fumes.

TIMER

A timer is useful when you are baking clay. Polymer clay requires a certain minimum baking time to set properly. Check the manufacturer's instructions. Baking for longer than the recommended time will not usually harm the clay, but some techniques require more precise timing.

THERMOMETER

A thermometer is vital to check the temperature of your oven as the oven's own thermostat may be unreliable.

BEAD ROLLERS

Sometimes you need to make many identical beads, and this is made easier with a bead roller. Bead rollers come in several bead shapes and sizes, including spheres, ovals, barrels, bicones, and fancy combination shapes (see page 47).

CLAY SHAPERS

Clay shapers are flexible, rubber-tipped tools that are used to shape clay. A pointed clay shaper is the most useful for finishing and neatening bead holes.

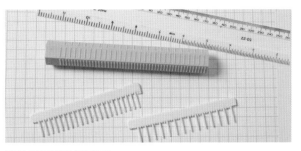

MEASURING TOOLS

Useful measuring tools include: ruler; graph paper—place this under a glass or clear acrylic work surface for instant measurements when cutting and measuring; notebook—useful for recording proportions, techniques, and ingredients as well as jotting down ideas.

A Marxit tool has six different sides that make indentations in a range of measurements onto a clay log, cane, or sheet.

Alternatively, break off the teeth of a comb at intervals to make a simple measuring tool.

CRAFT HEAT GUN

A craft heat gun can be used to "set" small areas of clay or liquid clay but not to fully cure or bake it.

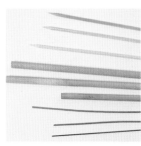

SKEWERS AND WIRES

Bamboo skewers and straight wires are used for baking beads on and are supported by a pair of stands so the clay does not touch the base of the baking tray. The beads can be varnished while still on the skewers.

POLYESTER FIBERFILL

Polyester fiberfill is useful for resting beads on during baking. It doesn't mark the clay, holds the shape of a shaped bead, and can withstand the baking temperature.

SANDPAPER

You will need waterproof (wet and dry) sandpaper in various grits. The lower the number, the coarser the grit. For most sanding purposes, 400- to 800-grit will be fine (see Sanding, page 48).

BUFFING WHEEL

A mechanical polisher with a cotton buffing wheel will give a professional finish to many styles of bead and will produce better effects than varnishing and hand polishing.

PROTECTION

Always wear a dust mask and eye protection when sanding or buffing beads. Tie back hair and remove any loose clothing.

▶ **SEE ALSO** ▶ Baking, page 17 ▶ Sanding and polishing, page 48

CONDITIONING

IT IS NECESSARY TO CONDITION POLYMER CLAY before you use it, whichever brand you choose, and even if it is a new block of clay. Conditioning remixes the color and PVC particles with the plasticizer, making the crumbly clay malleable and easier to work. It also removes tiny air pockets which, when heated, can leave an uneven surface on the baked bead.

You can condition clay either by kneading it, using the warmth of your skin to soften the clay, or it can be fed through a pasta machine. Note that conditioned clays will need reconditioning if left unused for several days.

> **TOOLS & MATERIALS**
> ● Polymer clay
> ● Tissue blade
> ● Brayer or acrylic roller
> ● Pasta machine

CONDITIONING CLAY BY HAND

You can easily condition a small amount of clay—enough for a few beads—by rolling it in your hands. Alternatively, you can roll the clay on your work surface; folding it in half, rolling, and twisting until it is soft. The clay is "conditioned" and ready to use when it is soft and malleable, and can be stretched and folded without cracking.

SLICING THE CLAY

Using a straight tissue blade, cut ⅛" (3 mm) slices from a block of clay. Lay about 10 slices vertically in a row on the work surface, overlapping them slightly.

ROLLING THE CLAY

Use a brayer or roller (if you don't have a roller, you can use a smooth-sided glass tumbler instead) to roll out the slices so they become flatter and blend into each other. Lift the clay off the work surface, fold in half, and roll the clay again. Roll and fold the clay several times until the clay becomes soft and pliable, ready for rolling into an even, thick sheet.

CONDITIONING CLAY USING A PASTA MACHINE

Rolling clay through a pasta machine is quicker and easier than kneading it by hand.

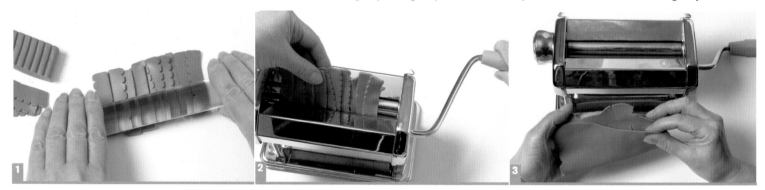

SLICING THE CLAY

Using a straight tissue blade, cut ⅛" (3 mm) slices from a block of clay. Lay about 10 slices vertically in a row, overlapping them slightly. Use a brayer or roller to roll out the clay until it is the thickness of the thickest setting on the pasta machine.

USING THE PASTA MACHINE

If necessary, trim the width of the sheet to fit the width of the pasta machine's rollers. Set the pasta machine on the thickest setting and roll the clay through. Fold the sheet in half, across the width, and roll through the pasta machine again, with the folded edge leading. This will stop air from becoming trapped inside the clay.

ROLLING THE CLAY

Continue to fold and roll the clay until it is soft and pliable. This usually takes 10 to 15 rolls and folds, depending on the brand of clay. The clay is "conditioned" and ready to use when it is soft and malleable and can be stretched and folded without cracking.

PROBLEMATIC CLAY

Polymer clay may be either too hard or soft to work with.

HARD CLAY

If your clay is old and hard, but has not been baked, it can be revitalized by chopping it up and mixing it with a small amount of polymer clay softener (always follow the manufacturer's mixing instructions), which will soften it without altering the color. Grating the old clay or using a food processor will speed the mixing process.

SOFT CLAY

The consistency of different-colored clays (even those made by the same manufacturer) can vary, so it may be necessary to "leach" the clay to make it firmer. Place the sheet of clay between two sheets of white paper, place a heavy weight on top, and leave overnight. The paper will absorb the excess plasticizer, resulting in firmer clay.

> ▶ **Tip**
> ▶ It is easier to condition your clay if it is warmed with a hairdryer or radiator, but be careful not to harden the clay by overheating it instead of softening it.

Thermometer

BAKING

BAKING, OR "CURING," IS AN ESSENTIAL PART of all polymer clay work. Heat causes the polyvinyl particles in the clay to polymerize, making the clay hard and strong. Under-baking will result in weakened clay and beads that may crack. Most clay brands recommend baking at 266°F/130°C for about 30 minutes, but baking for longer, or rebaking several times, does not seem to harm the clay. Always check the packet for baking instructions as temperatures and baking times can vary between brands.

Place the baking tray on the middle shelf of the oven for even heating. If you are baking tall pieces or think that your oven heats unevenly, then cover the tray with a "tent" of aluminum foil.

TEMPERATURE AND DURATION

Opinions about temperatures and baking times vary enormously, so experiment with the oven settings and the thermometer to find out what suits you and the beads you are baking. It is advisable to purchase an oven thermometer to help you check the oven settings.

BAKING BEADS

To stop beads from rolling around and sticking to each other on the baking tray, there are several ways you can

A variety of supports for beaking beads

separate and support them.

Beads can be placed on a bed of polyester fiberfill. The texture of this material will not impress on the beads and the temperature necessary for baking polymer clay is not high enough to melt the polyester fibers.

Bake flat beads on paper to prevent them from getting shiny spots from contact with metal, glass, or ceramic tiles. However, placing round beads on paper may leave a round flat mark on the bead.

Small round beads can be baked on a folded paper concertina to stop them from rolling around (see left). This method is best if you prefer to drill the thread hole after baking.

Beads with a thread hole can be threaded onto a wire or bamboo skewer and supported at each end on a stand (see left). This method is useful if the beads are textured. (If the cooled beads are difficult to remove from the skewer, put the skewer and beads back into a hot oven for a few moments and remove from the skewer while they are still warm.)

SUPPORTS

To make a stand, use a 1" (25 mm) thick "log" of scrap clay and cut off two pieces, each about 1¼" (30 mm) long. Stand each log on its end and use a bamboo skewer or similar tool to press across the clay to make a channel. Bake the two pieces standing upright.

You can make these stands any height you wish, so that large beads can be raised above the base of the baking tray as they bake.

OVENS

You can use a household oven to bake your beads in, but it is not recommended. If you make beads on a regular basis, you should invest in a small worktop oven dedicated to polymer clay use only. Many polymer clay artists use a toaster or convection oven. A fan-assisted oven ensures that the heat is circulated more evenly throughout the oven. If you do use a household oven, make a "tent" out of aluminum foil or use a lidded casserole or baking dish to prevent the plasticizer residue from being deposited on the oven walls.

You may notice a slight smell during baking; this is normal and harmless. However, it is sensible always to ventilate the workroom as when clay overheats, the fumes are unpleasant and possibly toxic. If possible, bake in a separate room to where you work.

Never try to bake your beads in a microwave oven.

COOLING

It does not seem to matter whether beads are left to cool slowly in the oven or removed while hot. Once baked, polymer clay remains pliable until it has cooled. This is a useful feature if you want to bend pieces and "set" them to a new shape while holding them under cold running water.

▶ **SEE ALSO** ▶ Using a pasta machine, page 14

MAKING LOGS, SNAKES, STRINGS, AND SHEETS

"LOG," "SNAKE," AND "STRING" are terms to describe the working thicknesses of clay. In this book, a "log" is any roll thicker than ⅜" (10 mm); a "snake" is any roll between ⅜" (10 mm) and ⅛" (3 mm); while a "string" is ⅛" (3 mm) or less.

It is a good idea to practice rolling a single piece of clay to make a thick log, then continue rolling it until you have made a very thin string.

SIZE DEFINITIONS

A log: thicker than ⅜" (10 mm)

A snake: ⅜" (10 mm)–⅛" (3 mm)

A string: ⅛" (3 mm) or thinner

> ▶ **Tip**
> ▶ When two different-colored clays are
> used and rolled together from a snake
> into a string, the twisting at the thin end
> shows as very fine lines and can be
> used as decoration on a bead.

ROLLING A "LOG"

Roll a ball of well-conditioned clay (see page 16) between the palms of your hands. Place the ball on the work surface and shape it into a thick log by rolling it on the work surface with your hands.

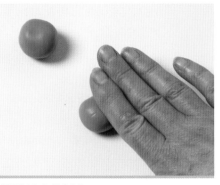

MAKING A "SNAKE"

Make the thick log thinner by rolling the clay backward and forward using your hand. Use both hands when both will fit on the log. As you roll, move your hands toward the ends of the clay. Gradually the clay log will get longer and thinner as it becomes a snake.

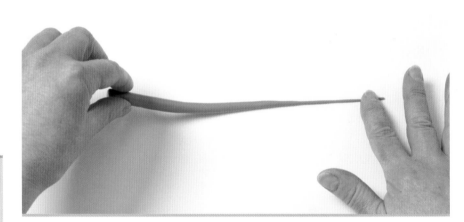

MAKING A "STRING"

Continue rolling the clay until it makes a thin string. Use the fingertips of one hand to roll the clay, at the same time raising the thick end of the clay up with your other hand, to take up slack as the string gets longer. Carefully pull the thinner portion out and away so you make a very thin string.

The three main thicknesses of clay: log, snake, and string. The bottom photo shows a snake becoming a string.

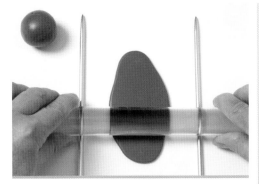

ROLLING A SHEET BY HAND

Roll a ball or log of well-conditioned clay (see page 16), place it on your work surface, and flatten it with the palm of your hand. Place a pair of knitting needles on either side of the clay. Roll the clay with a roller until it is thin enough that the roller is touching the knitting needles. The rolled clay sheet will be even and the same thickness as the needles. You can roll small sheets of clay of various thicknesses by using an assortment of knitting needles, dowels, or stacks of cards.

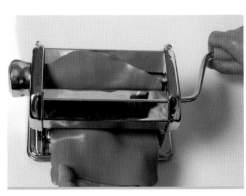

ROLLING A SHEET USING A PASTA MACHINE

It is much easier and quicker to roll clay sheets of even thickness using a pasta machine. Shape the conditioned clay into a thin rectangular slab or pancake, set the pasta machine to the thickest setting, and feed the sheet between the rollers while turning the handle. To make thinner sheets, reduce the setting by one step and re-roll. Keep doing this until the sheet reaches the desired thickness.

MEASURING LOGS AND SHEETS

There are several different ways of measuring clay logs and sheets for cutting into beads.

USING A MEASURE

Place a ruler or tape measure close to the log and mark off even portions along the log. Hold a tissue blade on the log and "walk" the blade through the clay to cut the marked portions. Let the log roll to avoid distorting it. Don't press down on the log or you will distort the clay and not get the same volume of clay in each bead.

> ### Tips
> ▶ To roll very thin sheets, sandwich the clay between sheets of baking paper. This stops the clay from tearing and sticking to the work surface. The technique also works well with a pasta machine.
>
> ▶ Put a sheet of graph paper underneath a glass work surface for an on-the-spot measure for cutting logs or sheets.
>
> ▶ If you do not have a Marxit tool, use a coarse hair comb to mark out the beads. If you want larger beads, break off the teeth of the comb at regular intervals to create different spacings (below).

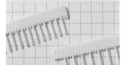

CUTTING

Use a cookie cutter to cut identical pieces from a rolled sheet of clay to then make into equal size beads. Alternatively, roll two, three, or more pieces of cut-out clay together to make gradated beads.

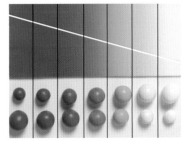

GRADATED BEADS

Cut out long, thin triangles from a sheet of clay and then divide them into equal-width portions to make gradated beads. Here, a Skinner blended sheet has been used to give a color gradation.

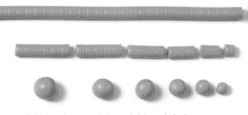

MARXIT TOOL

Polymer clay artist Donna Kato designed a clever measuring tool called a Marxit tool. It has six different sides with raised measurements ranging from ⅛–¾" (3–20 mm) on each side, which indent on the clay along a 6" (150 mm) log. You can use this to cut identically sized beads or gradated beads.

Roll a log of an even thickness, lightly mark the log with the Marxit tool and cut into identical portions for identical-sized beads, or cut incremental portions for gradated beads, and roll into balls.

▶ **SEE ALSO** ▶ *Cutting and slicing, page 28* ▶ *Caning and stacking, page 30*

COLOR MIXING

MIXING CLAY IS LIKE MIXING PAINT. With a few basic colors you can make and match a host of other colors. Some of these are available ready-mixed in most brands along with metallic, mica, pearl, and translucent polymer clays.

Mix in a touch of black to reduce the brightness of a colored clay or mix in an abundance of white to create pastel colors. The intensity of ready-made, store-bought colors varies enormously. Some, such as red, are overpowering in a mix, so use them sparingly. Tint translucent clay by adding a small amount of colored clay. Only mix colors a little at a time, and add the dark color to the light color, never the other way around.

Take notes of the proportions of the colors you used, so you can repeat a successful mix.

You can mix small amounts of clay by hand, but it is quicker and easier to use a pasta machine. Mixing is extremely important when making beads that imitate natural materials, such as coral and turquoise (see Faux Effects, pages 68–101).

BASIC PALETTE

Black/brown

Medium green

Cerulean blue

Cobalt blue

Mauve

Magenta

Cadmium orange

Cadmium yellow

White

A suggested basic palette

COLOR MIXING BY HAND

Mixing small amounts of colored clay is useful for carrying out color tests. It is quick and easy and means you won't end up with a very large amount of a disappointing color.

½" (12 mm)   ½" (12 mm)

A clay log marked into equal portions for controlled color mixing.

COMBINING COLORS

Roll two clays (here pink and blue have been used) into ½" (12 mm) diameter "logs" and mark into ½" (12 mm) portions using a ruler. Roll two portions of blue clay and four portions of pink clay into "snakes." Lay these snakes together, roll, and twist them into a log. The colors will begin to marble together. Fold the log in half and roll and twist again. Continue to roll, twist, and fold until the colors have mixed thoroughly.

If you do not like the color, add another piece of one of the colored clays and roll and twist again to mix the colors. Remember to keep a note of the color proportions you use. Any mixes that become mudlike can be revitalized by adding a metallic mica clay or can be used for bead cores.

▶ **Tips**
▶ Light colors are easy to ruin, so mix your light colors before the dark ones. Use wet hand wipes to keep hands, tools, and work surface clean, cleaning between colors.

▶ If a newly mixed color doesn't work, don't throw it in the garbage. Even muddy colors are useful; use them for a bead core.
▶ Warm clay is easier to mix.

MIXING COLORS

1 Roll and twist the colors to be mixed together.

2 Fold the log in half and twist the two ends together.

3 Continue folding in half and twisting until the colors blend.

MECHANICAL COLOR MIXING

Having made your test colors by hand, you can scale up the proportions to mix a large amount for bigger projects. Here, one part blue-green has been added to two parts of yellow to make a vibrant green.

Mixing a lot of clay is made much easier by using a food processor to chop up the clay and a pasta machine to thoroughly mix the colors and condition the clay at the same time.

CHOPPING THE CLAY

Measure out the proportions of clay you require. Chop the clay into chunks the size of sugar lumps and place in the food processor. Don't overfill the bowl or you may damage the motor. Operate the processor in short bursts to finely chop the clay and disperse the colors, but do not over-process so that the clay turns into a clump. The food processor will warm the clay a little and make rolling through the pasta machine easier.

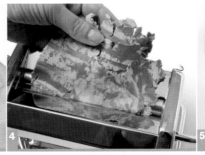

COMPRESSING THE CLAY

Empty the bowl of chopped clay onto the work surface and use a roller to compress the clay bits together.

MAKING A PANCAKE

Scrape the clay off the work surface with a spatula and pinch the clay to make a pancake that is a little thicker than the thickest setting on the pasta machine.

USING THE PASTA MACHINE

Roll the clay through the pasta machine. Keeping the pasta machine on its thickest setting, fold the clay sheet in half and roll it through with the folded edge leading. Continue to fold and roll the clay sheet until the colors are thoroughly mixed and there is no color streaking.

THE MIXED CLAY

The proportions of clay used and the sheet of thoroughly mixed colors.

COLOR BLENDING

A wide range of colors (right) can be made from the three basic primaries plus white. Try your own mixtures to get exactly the shade you require.

White

Cadmium yellow

Magenta

Cobalt blue

▶ **SEE ALSO** ▶ Using a pasta machine, page 14 ▶ Making logs and sheets, page 18

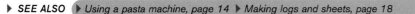

A necklace of tube beads made from a Skinner blend using navy blue and yellow.

BLENDING— THE SKINNER TECHNIQUE

THE SKINNER BLEND WAS DEVELOPED BY Judith Skinner, who found that different-colored clays could be combined together using a pasta machine so that they blended smoothly from one solid color to another. This technique has been used by polymer clay artists in a wide variety of ways ever since.

Before making a Skinner blend, see what the colors will look like when mixed together. To do this, mix equal small portions of the two colors by hand.

Skinner blends can be made of two or more colors, for example the multicolored rainbow Skinner blend uses a number of different-colored clays (see necklace, above).

TOOLS & MATERIALS
- Polymer clays of two or more colors
- Tissue blade
- Pasta machine

A necklace made from a Skinner blended log cut into beads using a ripple blade. The beads were threaded with a tiny seed bead between each.

1

ROLLING THE CLAY

Choose two different colored clays, for example yellow and red. Roll a sheet of each color on the thickest setting of a pasta machine. Using a tissue blade, cut the sheet into squares. Each square should be just less than the width of the pasta machine. With a tissue blade, make a diagonal cut across each square, 1" (25 mm) in from each corner. Dividing the colored sheets in this way will leave unmixed color at each end of the blend.

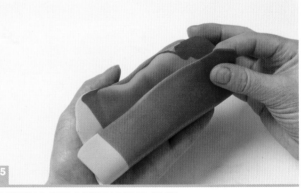

5

FOLDING AND ROLLING THE CLAY

Fold the clay sheet in half again and roll it through the pasta machine on the thickest setting, fold first.

Simple coil beads made from a rainbow-colored Skinner blend strung together with bought silver beads.

2

3

4

MERGING THE COLORS

Replace one of the red triangles with the corresponding yellow triangle so you form a square again. Put the other two triangles to one side.

BLENDING THE COLORS

Fold the two colored sheets back on themselves and press them together.

ROLLING THE CLAY

Place the folded edge of the clay in the pasta machine and roll through on the thickest setting.

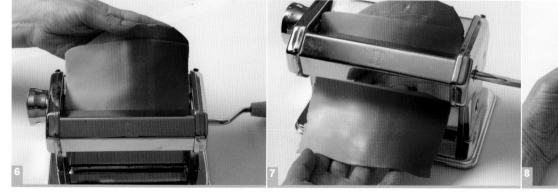

NEW COLOR APPEARS

Continue to fold and roll the clay another ten to fifteen times. Gradually the streaked colors will blend together creating another color, in this case orange. The clay sheet will become misshapen, but this is natural.

THE COLORS BLEND

The sheet of blended colors on the last roll through the pasta machine.

THE FINISHED SHEET

The Skinner blend is complete.

▶ **SEE ALSO** ▶ *Using a pasta machine, page 14* ▶ *Color mixing, page 20*

Large, round beads made with a core of lightweight clay, covered with a combed, patterned veneer, and strung with torn pieces of black clay imitating natural coco chips.

Tube beads of combed, patterned clay, threaded with brass beads, and natural coco chips dyed black *(right)*.

COMBING, FEATHERING, AND SWIRLING

WHEN YOU START TO MIX two or more clay colors to make a new blended color, very decorative streaks, swirls, and marbling quickly appear. Similar effects are found in glass and ceramic beads but are more easily achieved with polymer clay. There are endless possibilities whether you choose the random swirls of hand-rolled balls, the more controlled patterns of swirled lentils, or the traditional look of combed or feathered clay patterns. With liquid polymer clay, you can take the feathering effect to an almost painterly finish.

TOOLS & MATERIALS
- Polymer clay—equal amounts of gold, copper, silver mica, black and white
- Scrap clay
- Tissue blade
- Brayer or acrylic roller
- Blunt tapestry needle
- Pasta machine

COMBING
Combing is a decorative effect that works well on flat and shaped surfaces. Combed patterns are found in textiles, ceramics, painting, paper, glass, and even cake decoration, so it is no surprise to find the technique applied to polymer clay.

> ▶ **Tip**
> ▶ Using a base of scrap clay makes a thicker clay, which can withstand the scoring in the later steps.

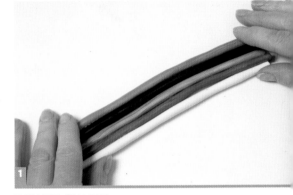

ROLLING SNAKES

Roll long snakes, about ¼" (6 mm) thick, using each of the colored clays (not the scrap clay). Lay the five snakes next to each other on the work surface.

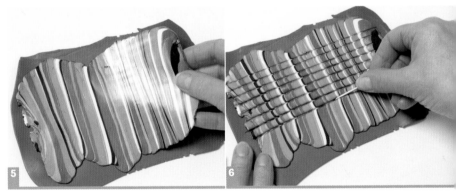

ADDING THE SCRAP CLAY

Roll out a thick sheet of scrap clay and lay the striped sheet on top of it. Smooth the clay with a roller or brayer to expel any trapped air bubbles.

SCORING THE CLAY

With a blunt tapestry needle, score parallel lines across the stripes. They should be just deep enough to drag and distort the lines in the clay, but do not score all the way through.

FORMING A LOG

Begin to roll the snakes together using your hands, letting them twist into a thick log. Cut the log in half using a tissue blade, lay the halves next to each other, and continue to roll and twist. To make more stripes, halve the log again, roll, and twist.

SHAPING THE LOG

When you have twisted and rolled the clay, and have made a log with many stripes, push the log in from both ends with your fingertips to make it the same length as the width of the pasta machine rollers.

ROLLING THE CLAY

Slightly flatten the log with the palm of your hand. Position the brayer or roller along the log and roll across the clay to lengthen the stripes. Roll the clay until it is the thickness of the thickest setting on the pasta machine. Place the clay in the pasta machine, with the stripes vertical to the rollers, and roll through.

COMBING THE CLAY

Turn the clay sheet around 180° and score between the first set of lines. This will form a feathered appearance as the clay is dragged in opposing directions.

RE-ROLLING THE CLAY

Set the pasta machine to the thickest setting, place the clay with the scored lines vertical to the rollers, and roll it through.

THE PATTERNED CLAY

The combed clay after being rolled through the pasta machine once. The clay is now ready for making into beads.

▶ **SEE ALSO** ▶ *Making logs and sheets, page 18* ▶ *Mixing colors, page 20* ▶ *Tube beads, page 43* ▶ *Sanding and polishing, page 48*

Irregular flat beads decorated with feathered liquid clay and threaded with rubber cord.

Reshaped lentil beads made with iridescent and pearl clays.

FEATHERING USING LIQUID POLYMER CLAY

Liquid polymer clays are useful for creating enamel-like decorative effects. There are several different types of liquid clay on the market, but here Kato Polyclay has been used as it flows and levels well, leaving a smooth surface finish.

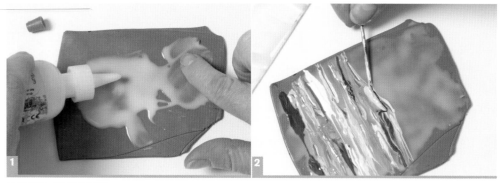

MAKING THE BASE

Roll out a sheet of scrap clay on a thick setting on a pasta machine. Liberally pour the liquid polymer clay onto the sheet and smear with your finger to cover the sheet.

ADDING OIL PAINT

Mix each color of oil paint with liquid polymer clay (in a 1:4 ratio) on a mixing palette. Apply to the clay in random stripes using a tapestry needle or similar tool.

MAKING THE FLAT BEADS

To make the flat beads, cut the unbaked feathered clay sheet while it is still on the tile, curving the tissue blade to cut the shapes. Remove any waste clay and bake the beads on the tile (see page 17).

Roll a sheet of medium thick black clay on the pasta machine. When the beads have cooled, place a bead face up on the sheet of black clay and, using the tissue blade, trim the black clay to ¼" (6 mm) all around the bead. Fold the black clay up and around the edge of the bead to form a frame and slice off the excess black clay level with the feathered surface using the tissue blade. Rebake the bead lying face up on a piece of paper.

When cool, wet-sand the back and edges of the bead, avoiding the feathered surface. Apply two coats of varnish to the feathered surface to give a glazed appearance.

TOOLS & MATERIALS

- Scrap polymer clay
- Liquid polymer clay, such as Kato Polyclay
- Oil paint in several colors
- Black polymer clay
- Pasta machine
- Mixing palette and stirrer
- Blunt tapestry needle or similar
- Large tile
- Tissue blade
- Piece of paper for baking
- 400–800-grit wet and dry sandpapers
- Varnish, such as Ranger's Poly-Glaze

MAKING A PATTERN

Use a blunt tapestry needle to lightly drag the oil paint through the liquid clay, making parallel lines ¼" (6 mm) apart across the whole sheet.

THE FEATHERED PATTERN

Turn the sheet around 180° and, working between the first set of lines, use the needle to drag the paint in the opposite direction. Place the sheet on a large tile and leave for a while to allow the liquid clay to flow and level itself. This will soften the appearance of the feathered lines.

A necklace of swirl beads with glitter clay shaped into points by pinching. The beads are threaded through the point and strung with disks of wood and metal.

SWIRLED BEADS

Swirled beads are fun to make; the ones shown here are made using the basic lentil shape (see page 39).

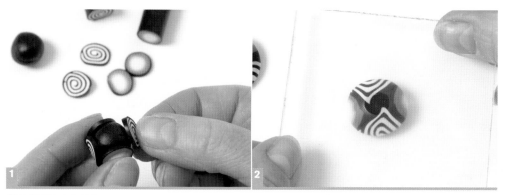

FORMING A BALL

Roll a ⅝" (15 mm) ball of black clay in the palms of your hands. Cut two thin slices from each of the canes using a tissue blade, then place them around the middle of the ball so the slices from the same canes are opposite each other. Press the slices onto the outside of the ball using your hands.

MAKING THE SWIRL PATTERN

Place the ball on a smooth work surface. Hold the piece of glass with both hands parallel to the work surface and on top of the ball. Rotate the glass in one direction. Gradually the pattern in the canes will start moving toward the center of the ball and a swirl will begin to form. Do not rush this process but continue to rotate the glass. Check the underside of the bead as there may be a more interesting pattern forming underneath. If you decide to work on the underside of the bead, turn the bead over and rotate the glass in the opposite direction.

RESHAPING THE BEADS

You can reshape the swirl beads simply by pinching them with your fingers. To make a square-shaped bead, press the sides of a lentil bead (see page 39) with your fingers and thumbs, then use two pieces of a square dowel to press against the sides of the bead to sharpen the square shape.

TOOLS & MATERIALS

- Black polymer clay
- Two different "canes" about ½" (12 mm) diameter (see page 30)
- Tissue blade
- Small piece of glass with blunt edges, or a flat-based glass tumbler
- Square dowels (for reshaping)

Lentil-shaped beads with swirls, formed from two slices of a black and gold jelly roll cane placed around a ball of black clay. Each bead is fitted with an eye pin and hangs from a rubber cord threaded with gold metal coils.

▶ **SEE ALSO**   ▶ Lentil beads, page 39   ▶ Varnishing, page 49

Black-and-white jigsaw beads joined along the rippled curves and cut into cubes.

A necklace of daisy beads strung through one petal and threaded with silver balls.

A few pink-and-white daisies; cut with two different cookie cutters.

CUTTING AND SLICING

MANY OF THE DECORATIVE EFFECTS and variations possible with polymer clay derive from different ways of cutting up the material. Polymer clay artists have adopted cutting tools from medical and other professions to add to more conventional craft knives.

Tissue blades are thin, flexible, and very sharp knives used in pathology. The blades are now available from craft and polymer clay suppliers along with ripple blades and craft knives. Replace tissue blades when they become blunt as a dulled blade will drag the clay and distort a cane slice.

Cookie cutters are incredibly useful cutting tools, and many different shapes are available from specialized catering stores. Cookie cutters cut through polymer clay easily whether made of metal or plastic.

TOOLS & MATERIALS
- Polymer clay—any color
- Roller or pasta machine
- Needle tool
- Tissue blade

FACET

Facet beads look best with crisp edges and flat faces so make sure you use a really sharp blade and cool the clay to ensure that it doesn't distort when cut.

MAKING A STACK

Roll out the clay into thick sheets using a roller or pasta machine. Make a 10-layer stack of the sheets, then leave it to rest.

When the clay stack is cool and firm, cut it into small blocks about 1" (25 mm) high by ⅝" (15 mm) wide. Lightly mark the long edges of a clay block into three equal parts, using the needle tool, then mark the edges of the top and bottom of the block into halves.

Stand the block upright and line up the markings on the bottom and long edges to make a corner. With the tissue blade held at an angle to the work surface, cut off the corner of the block. Cut off the other three corners in the same way, then turn the piece over to cut off the corners at the other end.

Make the thread hole through the bead with a needle tool. Bake the beads (see page 17).

Facet beads with a metallic finish.

DAISY

Cookie cutters lend themselves to color design games in this delightfully simple bead.

TOOLS & MATERIALS
- Polymer clay—white, black, and yellow
- Pasta machine
- Tissue blade
- Flower cookie cutters— large and small
- Ball stylus
- Needle tool
- Piece of paper for baking

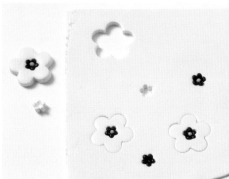

CREATING THE FLOWERS

Roll out the white and then the black clay on the thickest setting of the pasta machine. Using a tissue blade, cut each sheet in half, then stack one half on top of the other to make double-thickness sheets of each color.

Using the small cookie cutter, cut out and remove a flower shape from the center of the white clay (this will become the black flower center). Repeat this in the black clay to make a small black flower (which will become the white flower center).

Place the black flower into the white clay cut-out shape and the white flower into the black clay

Black-and-white Vera beads made from a thin, layered stack, and cut with a cookie cutter to reveal stripes at the edge.

A Vera bead necklace using a Skinner blend of pigmented and metallic mica clays.

cut-out shape. Use a ball stylus to gently press in the center of each small flower to make a small dimple.

Roll tiny balls of the yellow clay and place one in each flower center dimple. Be careful not to flatten the balls or the surrounding clay.

Place the large cookie cutter centrally over the black flower on the white sheet and cut out the clay, but don't remove the cut-out. Repeat on the black sheet for the other flower.

Continue to make more flowers in both the black and white sheets. When all the flowers have been made, remove the clay surrounding each flower. Removing the clay at the end avoids distorting any of the flowers.

Make the thread hole across a petal of each flower bead using the needle tool. Place the beads flat on a piece of paper and bake (see page 17).

VERA BEADS

Cookie cutters are useful for making identical shapes, as in these Vera beads.

TOOLS & MATERIALS
- Maroon polymer clay
- Copper mica polymer clay
- Tissue blade
- 1¼" (3 mm) triangular cookie cutter
- Needle tool
- Tile for baking
- 400–800-grit wet and dry sandpapers
- Buffing cloth or buffing wheel (optional)

MAKING THE BEADS

This sophisticated effect has been made with a Skinner blend (see page 22) of maroon clay and copper mica clay. Cut the blend in half lengthways and stack it so the colors match and the stack is at least ³⁄₁₆" (6 mm) thick.

Cut out triangles using the cookie cutter, positioning the cutter so that the color of the blend flows through the beads from the wide end to the point of the triangle.

Use the point of the cookie cutter to cut out a small V shape in the middle of the wide end of the triangle. Use a tissue blade to neaten the edges if necessary.

Use a needle tool to make the thread hole through the bead from the small V to the point of the triangle and bake flat on a tile (see page 17). After baking, wet-sand the bead to sharpen the edges of the V shape, and polish to enhance the shimmer effect of the mica particles.

JIGSAW BEADS

Jigsaw beads exploit the decorative possibilities of an unsual craft blade and the way that raw polymer clay bonds to itself without adhesive.

TOOLS & MATERIALS
- Polymer clay—black and white
- Pasta machine
- Ripple blade
- Straight tissue blade
- Needle tool

MAKING AND CUTTING A STACK

Roll out black and white clay sheets on the thickest setting of the pasta machine. Make separate black and white stacks eight layers thick—they should be about ¾" (18 mm) high by 3" (75 mm) long by 1½" (37 mm) wide. Use a ripple blade to cut across each stack at a 45° angle.

MAKING A CUBE

Carefully push together half the white stack and half the black stack, matching the ripples of the cut. Cut the edges of the piece into a cube with a straight tissue blade. Use a needle tool to make the thread hole across the center of the bead between a black corner and a white corner.

▶ **SEE ALSO** ▶ *Using a pasta machine, page 14* ▶ *Baking, page 17*

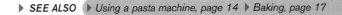

Various jelly roll cane designs.

A necklace of slices of a jelly roll cane from large to small, threaded with round, gradated red beads.

CANING AND STACKING

THE TERM "CANE" COMES FROM GLASSMAKING and refers to a glass rod with a pattern inside that runs from one end to the other. Millefiori or "thousand flowers" canes are made by assembling many small colored rods to form a large patterned cane. When this is heated and stretched, the pattern inside maintains a miniature version of the original, however narrow the cane becomes.

To build any complex canes you first need to make the simple basic canes. The most useful simple canes are the jelly roll, bull's eye, striped, and checked canes.

TOOLS & MATERIALS

JELLY ROLL
- Polymer clay—white and black
- Pasta machine
- Tissue blade
- Brayer or acrylic roller

BULL'S EYE CANE
- Polymer clay—white and black
- Pasta machine
- Tissue blade
- Needle tool
- Piece of paper for baking

JELLY ROLL CANE

Use contrasting colored clays to clearly show the jelly-roll pattern. Alternatively, make a jelly roll with a Skinner blend sheet (see page 22) for a cane where the color changes smoothly from the outside to the inside.

ROLLING THE CLAY

Roll out two sheets of clay, one white and one black, on the thickest setting of the pasta machine. Using a tissue blade, cut both sheets into 6 x 2½" (150 x 65 mm) rectangles and lay the white sheet on top of the black. Using a brayer or roller, smooth the sheets to expel any air pockets.

SHAPING THE SHEETS

Cut both short ends of the sheet at an angle with the tissue blade to reveal the black sheet underneath.

MAKING THE JELLY ROLL

Using your fingertips, roll the sheet up to make a tight jelly roll. Continue to roll to the end of the sheet, making sure that the white sheet is completely covered by the black sheet. Roll the cane on the work surface with both hands to make it more compact.

TRIMMING THE JELLY ROLL

Use a tissue blade to reveal the pattern. Cut slices for beads, reduce the size for use as onlays, or set aside to use in a more complex cane later.

RESHAPING THE JELLY ROLL

Jelly roll canes can be shaped into triangular or square canes. Pinch along the cane to form the angles. Use a roller to roll along the sides smoothing out the pinch marks.

Necklace made of bull's eye cane beads with rainbow-colored spacer beads.

REDUCING A CANE

"Reducing" is the process of stretching a large patterned cane. Some polymer clay artists make elaborate canes that are several inches in diameter before they reduce them.

To make a range of cane sizes, cut chunks off the cane at different stages of reduction. Wherever you cut a slice from a reduced cane, the image will be exactly the same with no loss of definition. Large canes tend to twist as they are reduced, so you may need to make a registration mark along the full length of the cane to help keep it straight as you reduce it. You can use a very thin line of translucent clay as this will disappear when the clay is baked.

DIFFERENT-SIZED SLICES

Slices cut from the jelly roll cane at different stages of reduction.

> ▶ **Tip**
> ▶ As there is a certain amount of distortion during the reduction process, some artists reduce each component before assembling a cane when making a complex cane. This avoids the need to reduce the cane further.

BULL'S EYE CANE

This basic cane is used in the Malachite technique (see page 92). It is also used for the foxglove flower bead (see page 46), where a single bull's eye cane is reduced, cut, and restacked several times to make a spotted cane.

STARTING TO REDUCE THE CANE

Make a jelly roll cane. Leave the cane to rest so all the clay becomes the same temperature. Begin to reduce the cane by pinching around the middle with your fingertips, to form an hourglass shape. Work your fingers toward the ends of the cane, pinching and rotating as you go. When reducing a larger cane, the ends may disappear inside the cane or the clay on the outside may run out as it becomes warmer and softer from handling. This is normal.

PINCHING THE CANE

Pinch around the end of the cane. Keep alternating from one end of the cane to the other. Once you have reduced the cane to the size you require, roll the cane on the work surface to smooth out any pinch marks. You can cut chunks or slices off the cane at any point during the reduction, to keep for later use, before you reduce the cane further.

ROLLING THE CANE

Roll some white clay into a log 3" (75 mm) long and ½" (12 mm) in diameter. Roll the black clay into a sheet on the thickest setting of the pasta machine. Using a tissue blade, cut the sheet into a strip 3" (75 mm) wide and lay the log across one end. Trim the front edge so that it is straight, and roll up the log until the front edge touches and marks the sheet. Slightly unroll the log and cut along the mark. Butt the join neatly.

Repeat the process with a sheet of white clay. Continue, alternating black and white sheets. Set the cane aside to use in a complex cane, or cut slices for beads, and using a needle tool, make a thread hole across the bead. Bake them flat on a piece of paper.

Cube beads made from colored, layered stacks.

STRIPED AND CHECKED CANES

Striped and checked are two basic patterns of canes. Striped canes can be made using rolled sheets of any thickness, and the stripes show best when contrasting colored clays are used. Thin slices from these canes can then be used as veneers or thick slices can be cut to form solid beads. A checked cane is a variation that begins as a striped cane.

RIBBON WEAVE BEADS

Like many polymer clay designs, these ribbon weave beads are a development of an idea by other polymer clay artists.

1

ROLLING THE CLAY

Roll out sheets of two contrasting colors on the thickest setting of a pasta machine. Using a tissue blade, cut each sheet in half and stack the halves to make double-thickness sheets of each color. Cut each sheet in half again and trim into a 1½ x 3" (37 x 75 mm) rectangle. Stack the sheets, alternating the colors to make a striped cane.

2

SLICING THE STRIPED CANE

Using a brayer or roller, smooth the stack to expel any air pockets. Using a tissue blade, cut long slices from the stack the same thickness as the bands of the stack—about ⅛" (3 mm).

3

MAKING THE CHECKED CANE

Stack the slices, alternating the colors of each layer to form a checked pattern. Using a roller, smooth the cane to compress the layers. The cane can be sliced at this point and used as beads or a border can be added (see below).

MAKING THE CANE

Roll out white and then black clay into medium thick sheets using a pasta machine. Lay the white sheet on top of the black sheet. Place one of the blended sides of the cane on top of the white sheet and trim the edges using a tissue blade. Repeat for the other side of the cane so the cane is covered in black clay.

ADDING A BORDER

To make a border, roll out a sheet of black clay on a medium to thin setting on the pasta machine. Place the cane on top of the sheet and trim the excess clay along the long sides using a tissue blade. Gently press the sheet onto the cane. Repeat for the other three sides. Set the cane aside to use in a complex cane later, or to make beads, cut ⅛" (3 mm) slices. Using the needle tool, make the thread hole from one corner of the bead to the other. Bake the beads lying flat on paper (see page 17). To finish, wet-sand and buff.

4

A ribbon weave necklace with store-bought curved silver tube beads.

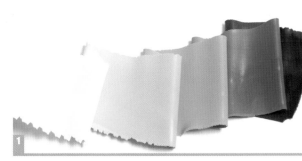

MAKING AND RE-ROLLING A SKINNER BLEND

Make a Skinner blend (see page 22) with all four colors. Roll the sheet out on the thickest setting of the pasta machine.

Using a tissue blade, cut a 2" (50 mm) strip across the colored blend. Reduce the setting on the pasta machine and roll the clay through lengthways. Reduce the setting again and roll through the clay. Repeat until the Skinner blend is long and thin.

MAKING PLEATS

Place the darker end of the blend on the work surface, then fold the strip back on itself in a concertina or fan-fold fashion, making a 1" (25 mm) pleat. Smooth the clay with your hand to sharpen the fold and to expel any air pockets. Continue to fold back and forth, smoothing the blend until all the clay has been pleated.

CUTTING THE STACK

Smooth the stack carefully with a roller to press the layers together without distorting it. Cut along the length of the stack with a tissue blade and place the two pieces together, with the white clay in the middle.

ROLLING THE CANE

Trim the ends using the tissue blade. Use a brayer or roller to lengthen and compress the cane until it is about ⅜" (10 mm) wide and 1" (25 mm) long.

SLICING THE CANE

Using a tissue blade, cut thin slices from the cane: you will need six slices for each bead. Roll a ⅝" (15 mm) ball of black clay and lay the slices around it, butting the ends to the edges so that the slices appear to weave over and under each other.

FINISHING THE BEADS

Using a knitting needle or clay shaper, press the edges of the slices into the black core ball to remove any ridges. This may distort the ball, so roll it in the palms of your hands to reshape it. Make a thread hole with the needle tool and bake the beads resting on a layer of polyester fiberfill (see page 17).

After baking, wet-sand the beads. Finish by buffing with a piece of denim for a satin finish or use a buffing wheel for a high shine.

▶ SEE ALSO   ▶ Using a pasta machine, page 14   ▶ Skinner blends, page 22   ▶ Cutting and slicing, page 28

A necklace using slices from two jelly rolls made from the same Skinner blend.

Beads made with slices of a kaleidescope cane formed over a baked bead core of scrap clay, taking care to match the pattern at the join.

SKINNER BLEND JELLY ROLL

Substituting sheets of colored blends for plain colors adds interest and subtlety to basic jelly roll canes.

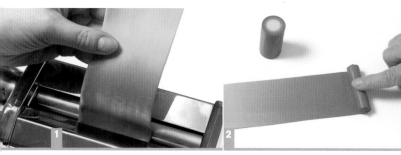

ROLLING THE CLAY

Fold the Skinner blend clay sheet in half as you did when rolling the blend but put it in the pasta machine with the end (not side) first. This will elongate the blended clay. Reduce the setting on the pasta machine by one and roll the clay through without folding the sheet in half. The blended clay will get longer and become rather unmanageable, but continue reducing the setting and rolling until you reach a thin setting. The thinner you roll the clay, the smoother the color blending will be.

MAKING THE JELLY ROLL

Place the long, blended sheet on the work surface, cut it in half lengthways with a tissue blade, and trim to neaten the ends and edges of both strips. Take one half, and roll up the clay from one end to form a jelly roll. With the other half, roll from the opposite end to make a jelly roll with a different colored center.

Alternatively, try rolling the Skinner blended sheet with a solid color, as below.

KALEIDOSCOPE CANES

Kaleidoscope canes look complicated to make even though the process is quite easy.

This cane began with a simple arrangement of colored logs and basic canes. The process of reducing, dividing, reassembling, and reducing again resulted in a rich and intricate cane.

Use canes as veneers or as the basis for beads such as lentil swirls.

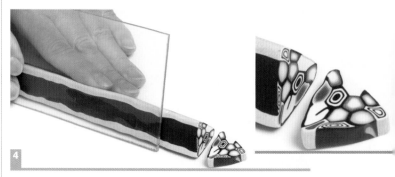

MAKING A TRIANGULAR SHAPE

Following the lines on the outside of the cane, use your fingertips to pinch along the cane to shape it into an equilateral triangle. Make two more pinch lines to form the triangle. Use a small piece of glass to flatten the sides of the triangular cane. Trim both ends of the cane using a tissue blade.

FORMING THE CANE

Roll a medium-thick sheet of black clay using a pasta machine. Stack canes as shown above. For added texture, slash one of the white logs along its length and insert the sheet of black clay into the cut. Wrap the remainder of the black sheet part of the way around the bundle of logs and trim all the logs to the same length using a tissue blade.

REDUCING THE CANE

Begin to reduce the cane by squeezing the cane in the middle to form an hourglass shape (see Reducing a cane, page 31). Use your fingers to pinch and squeeze the cane to reduce its diameter to half its original size.

ROLLING THE CANE

Begin rolling the cane on the work surface to lengthen the cane and to smooth out any bumps or ridges caused by the pinching. Keep the lines on the outside of the cane straight as you roll. The ends of the roll may become obscured, but you can reveal the cane pattern by slicing off the ends when the rolling is completed.

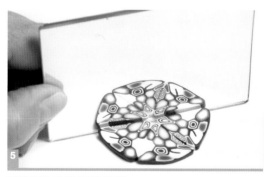

MAKING THE PATTERN

Cut three slices from the end of the cane and place them together, matching the pattern. Use a small mirror to view a full image of different combinations of your three slices. Note how the white log with the black line has added a graphic look.

COMPLETING THE PATTERN

Select the arrangement you prefer, cut the triangular cane into six equal portions, and join them together, taking care to match the pattern at both ends.

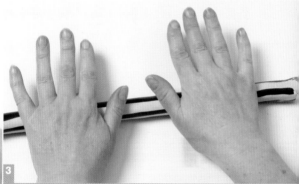

REDUCING THE CANE

To make beads, you need to reduce the cane in size again.

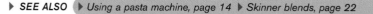

▶ **SEE ALSO** ▶ *Using a pasta machine, page 14* ▶ *Skinner blends, page 22*

MOLDING

MOLDED-BEAD SHAPES can be replicated from found objects, existing beads, or from patterns you make yourself. The molds for intricate shapes are made from proprietary silicone molding compounds or extra flexible polymer clay. Ordinary scrap polymer clay may be used to make shallow press molds. Very intricate beads can be cast from rubber molds, using clay softened by mixing in a little liquid clay—a material that is also ideal for imitating cloisonné work.

CLOISONNÉ

Here, a rubber stamp with a design of raised lines has been used so that the cast cloisonné beads also have raised lines.

Two molds have been made using the rubber stamp, and the cloisonné beads have been made by squeezing a ball of clay between the two molds, creating a bead that is decorated on both sides.

1

MAKING THE MOLDS

To make the two molds of the rubber stamp, roll out the scrap clay into a sheet on the thickest setting of the pasta machine. Cut the sheet in half using a tissue blade and stack the sheets together. Cut the sheet in half again and trim the edges of both pieces.

Spray the rubber stamp with water. Place one of the clay sheets onto the rubber stamp and firmly press the clay into the stamp with your fingertips. Carefully remove the impressed clay and lay it face up on a flat surface ready for baking. Make an identical second mold and bake both (see page 17).

TOOLS & MATERIALS

CLOISONNÉ

- Scrap polymer clay (enough for two molds and beads)
- Gold powder
- Pasta machine
- Tissue blade
- Rubber stamp with scroll pattern
- Water in a spray bottle
- Needle tool
- Soft paintbrush
- Dust mask
- Piece of paper for baking
- Water-based acrylic floor polish
- Mixing palette and stirrer
- Transparent liquid polymer clay, such as Kato Polyclay
- Oil paint in one or more colors

CINNABAR PENDANT

- Scrap clay for the mold
- Polymer clay—red and black
- Rubber cord made from a polymer clay such as Bake and Bend, ⅛" (3 mm) diameter
- Pasta machine
- Tissue blade or craft knife
- Water in a spray bottle
- Release agent
- Small piece of glass or a smooth tile
- 400–800-grit wet and dry sandpapers
- Piece of denim or buffing wheel (optional)

CINNABAR PENDANT

Cinnabar lacquer is associated with Eastern art, but this design uses loosely knotted rubber cord to generate abstract marks with the feel of a brushed script.

1

ROLLING THE CLAY

Roll the scrap clay into a sheet on the thickest setting on the pasta machine. Cut the sheet into three pieces using a tissue blade, lay them on top of each other, and trim to make a 2 x 3" (50 x 75 mm) rectangle. Using two or three lengths of cord, braid or tie a series of loose knots. Spray the clay with water and press the braid into it.

2

BAKING THE MOLD

Carefully remove the braid without distorting the impressed image. Trim the edges of the impressed block and bake it lying flat (see page 17). While the mold is baking, make the cinnabar-layered clay.

Begin by rolling out sheets of red and black clay on the thickest setting of the pasta machine.

Two Cinnabar pendants using a red
and a black layered clay for a different
appearance. The rubber cord is threaded
through coil beads; the center one is
secured to the top of the pendant.

IMPRESSING THE CLAY

When the baked molds have cooled,
spray both with water. Roll some
scrap clay into ½" (12 mm) balls or
larger. Place one ball between the
two molds, like the filling in a
sandwich, and press the top mold
down evenly to impress the image
into both sides of the clay ball and
to create a circular disk.

THE IMPRESSED DISK

Separate the two molds and check that
the impressed clay is well-defined on
both sides. You can make a thread hole
with a needle tool at this stage or drill
the hole when the beads have been
baked and finished.

PAINTING ON THE GOLD POWDER

Wear a dust mask to avoid breathing
in the dust particles. Use a soft
paintbrush to apply gold pearl
powdered pigment to the whole bead.
Bake the beads, resting on a piece of
paper (see page 17). When cool, seal
with a thin coating of water-based
floor polish.

APPLYING THE OIL PAINT

On a mixing palette, color the
transparent liquid polymer clay with a
little oil paint. Use a disposable stirrer
to mix and then transfer the liquid color
onto the bead. Working on one side of
the bead, use the point of a needle
tool to manipulate the paint into tight
corners. Bake, then repeat the coloring
process on the other side.

FORMING THE CINNABAR LAYERS

Cut a red sheet into a 2 x 3" (50 x 75 mm)
rectangle and place on top of the black sheet. Trim
the edges and roll through the pasta machine on the
thickest setting. Cut the sheet in half and place one
half on top of the other, keeping the alternating
color sequence. Roll through the pasta machine.
Repeat the process two more times (to make eight
layers of each color), but after the last stacking don't
roll the clay through the pasta machine.

IMPRESSING THE CLAY

When the baked mold has cooled,
spray it with water (or other release
agent). Firmly press either the red
or the black side of the layered
sheet into the mold—choose which
you prefer as the end result is very
different (see right).

TRIMMING AND SANDING THE PENDANT

Place the molded clay impressed side up on a small
piece of glass or a tile. With a tissue blade or craft knife,
trim the edge of the clay at an angle to
reveal the layers below. Bake the clay
flat on the glass or tile. Wet-sand the
piece to reveal some of the underlying
color. For a satin finish, buff with a piece
of denim or use a buffing wheel for a lacquered look.
Use a varnish of your choice if you prefer.

▶ **SEE ALSO**   ▶ *Baking, page 17*   ▶ *Attaching findings, page 108*

Rounds—
the most
useful of all bead shapes.

A necklace of faux
terra-cotta disk
beads.

BEAD SHAPES

IT IS TEMPTING to claim that any bead shape made from other materials can also be made using polymer clay—there seems to be no limits to its versatility. The infinite variations and possibilities means that polymer clay may also be used to generate unique shapes such as corkscrews and pleated beads. By combining techniques such as sculpting and caning, you can invent colorful confections that refer to nature (see the Trumpet bead on page 46), without imitating them exactly. The selection of shape-making techniques in this chapter merely skims the range of possible forms.

BASIC ROUND BEADS

Making round beads of consistent size and shape is an essential skill.

TOOLS & MATERIALS

- Polymer clay
- Sheet of glass
- Graph paper
- Tissue blade or craft knife
- Needle tool
- Piece of paper for baking

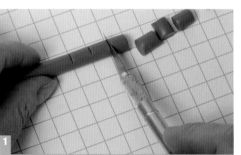

MAKING AND CUTTING A LOG

Make a log of even thickness by rolling some clay under a sheet of glass, held level on a smooth work surface. Using a craft knife, mark off equal spacings on the log; the graph paper ensures accuracy. Cut equal-sized pieces from the clay log.

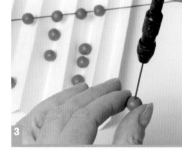

SHAPING

Put a measured piece of clay in your palm, cover with the other hand, and firmly rotate the top hand a few times, gradually easing pressure as the ball takes shape. Use your fingertips to "feel" for the final roundness of the bead.

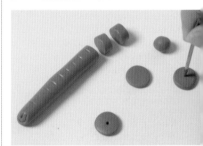

BAKING ROUNDS

Make the thread hole by piercing the bead with a needle, twisting rather than pushing, until the needle tip just exits the other side. Turn the bead and retwist into the exit hole. Bake the beads on a simple tray made out of folded paper to keep the beads from rolling around or on a skewer.

BASIC HANDMADE DISK

These disks are useful as spacer beads and are easy to make. They have a softer look than disk beads that have been cut out using a cookie cutter (see page 40).

TOOLS & MATERIALS

- Polymer clay
- Ruler
- Tissue blade or craft knife
- Tapestry needle
- Tile or piece of card stock for baking

MEASURING OUT THE DISKS

Roll a ½" (12 mm) thick log of polymer clay (see page 18). Using a ruler, mark the log into same-size portions. Cut off the portions using a tissue blade or craft knife and roll into round balls in the palms of your hands. Press down on a ball with your finger or thumb to flatten the ball into a disk.

Use a tapestry needle to make a thread hole through the center of the disk. Bake the disk flat on a tile or piece of card stock (see page 17).

Oval beads formed from various pink clays mixed with glitters.

A marbled teardrop.

A tetrahedron with soft edges.

Lentils—note the different positions of the threadholes.

OVAL

It takes practice to make oval beads that are consistently the same shape, but it is worth persevering at this.

TOOLS & MATERIALS
- Polymer clay
- Polyester fiberfill
- Needle tool
- Small tile or similar material

ROLLING THE BEADS

Measure out portions of clay that are the same size and roll them in your hands to make into balls. Continue to rotate the ball between the palms of your hands, always rotating in the same direction, until an oval shape forms. It can be flattened into a bun or lozenge shape.

Make a thread hole with the needle tool by piercing the oval from point to point or across the width of the bead. Bake the beads on polyester fiberfill (see page 17).

TEARDROP

The "teardrop" is a simple variation on a basic hand-rolled round bead. It looks especially good when polished or varnished.

TOOLS & MATERIALS
- Polymer clay
- Polyester fiberfill
- Needle tool

FORMING A TEARDROP

Roll the clay into ½" (12 mm) balls. Place a ball in the palm of one hand and place the edge of your other hand across the top of the ball. Slide your hand backward and forward across the bead to form a point. Make a thread hole with a needle tool across the point of the teardrop, or make it through the base of the bead, exiting through the point. Bake the beads on a piece of polyester fiberfill (see page 17).

BICONE AND LENTIL

It is hard to believe that such perfect shapes come from such a simple technique—try it and see!

TOOLS & MATERIALS
- Polymer clay
- Small piece of glass with blunt edges, or a flat-bottomed glass tumbler

ROLLING THE BEADS

Roll a ½" (12 mm) ball of clay in your hands and place it on a smooth work surface. Place a small piece of glass on top of the ball, parallel to the work surface, and rotate it in one direction. Gradually, a bicone will form. You can make different-shaped bicones—either more pointed or more flat—by varying how wide you make the rotations. Rotating the glass with just small movements will result in a lentil shape. In the background are two different-shaped bicones and a lentil bead.

TETRAHEDRON

This four-sided shape can be used to make dramatic jewelry.

TOOLS & MATERIALS
- Polymer clay
- Small piece of glass
- Needle tool
- Piece of paper for baking
- 400–800-grit wet and dry sandpapers

MAKING A TETRAHEDRON

Roll a ¾" (18 mm) diameter ball of clay in your hands. Pinch the clay between the index finger and thumb of both hands to form the clay into a four-sided shape (a tetrahedron).

STRAIGHTENING THE EDGES

Press the clay shape against a smooth, flat surface, such as a piece of glass, held at a 60° angle to the work surface. Turn the clay and press another side of the bead flat against the glass. Continue turning the clay and pressing each side of the bead against the glass until all the sides are flat and well formed.

Make a hole with the needle tool, entering the center of one edge and exiting at the center of the opposite edge. Bake the beads flat on a piece of paper (see page 17). Wet-sand the beads to enhance their shape.

▶ **SEE ALSO** ▶ *Baking, page 17* ▶ *Making logs and sheets, page 18* ▶ *Cutting and slicing, page 28*

Heart-shaped beads.

Cookie-cutter disks and a bead made from different-sized disks.

Folded disks made from a Skinner blend.

HEART

Hearts are always popular beads built on the basic lentil shape (see page 39). Practice to make the same shape each time or deliberately vary the size and color to show that every heart is unique.

TOOLS & MATERIALS
- Polymer clay
- Small piece of glass with blunt edges or a flat-bottomed glass tumbler
- Stiff piece of card stock or a credit card
- Needle tool
- Polyester fiberfill

ROLLING A LENTIL BEAD

Roll the clay into ½" (12 mm) and ¾" (18 mm) diameter balls. Place a ball on a smooth work surface. Firmly hold a piece of glass or a tumbler base over the ball and rotate in one direction to form the ball into a lentil shape.

INDENTING THE CLAY

Using a stiff piece of card stock or a credit card, push into the edge of the lentil to indent it and form a rough heart shape. Cover the credit card with a folded piece of paper to create more drag as you push it into the clay.

SHAPING THE HEART

Shape the bottom of the heart with your fingers to make a slight point. Make a thread hole across the widest part of the bead with the needle tool and bake resting on polyester fiberfill (see page 17). For earrings and pendants, make a hole at the top of the heart for an eye pin.

COOKIE-CUTTER DISK

Cookie-cutter disks have a crisp, clean shape that makes them useful spacer beads between more rounded fancy beads. Most are cut out of sheets rolled on the thickest setting of the pasta machine. As they can be repeated easily, the disks are useful where a design calls for large numbers of identical beads. They can be combined with disks of other sizes and colors for a variety of decorative beads.

TOOLS & MATERIALS
- Polymer clay
- Pasta machine
- ¾" (18 mm) cookie cutter
- Bamboo skewer
- Needle tool
- Polyester fiberfill

FOLDED DISK

Roll clay on the thickest setting of the pasta machine and then stamp out disks with a sharp cookie cutter. Curve the disks around a bamboo skewer.

Remove the disk from the skewer and make the thread hole through the two halves of the folded bead using a needle tool. Bake on a bed of polyester fiberfill.

A necklace of folded cookie-cutter disks made from a Skinner blend and threaded with silver spacer beads.

Saddle beads.

Donut beads—plain and with a metallic finish.

A coil bead made of a Skinner blend.

A coiled coil bead using a mix of several colors.

A chain link of twisted, multicolored clay.

SADDLE BEAD

This disk bead can either be cut out from a sheet of clay with a cookie cutter or sliced from a round cane.

TOOLS & MATERIALS

- Polymer clay
- Pasta machine
- Cookie cutter
- Tissue blade
- Needle tool
- Skewer (optional)
- Polyester fiberfill (optional)

MAKING A SADDLE BEAD

Roll out a sheet of medium-thick clay using a pasta machine and then cut disks from the clay using a cookie cutter. Alternatively, cut slices from a round cane (see page 30) using a tissue blade. Make the saddle bead by gently bending the disk forward and backward at the same time. This will curve the disk in the center so the edges curl up.

Make a thread hole through the center of the bead with a needle tool and bake threaded on a straight skewer or resting on polyester fiberfill.

COIL AND DONUT

Both coil and donut beads (a variation of a coil bead) are very effective beads to use for jewelry.

TOOLS & MATERIALS

- Polymer clay
- Bamboo skewer or similar tool
- Tissue blade
- Polyester fiberfill

MAKING A COIL BEAD

To make a coil bead, make a snake ¼" (6 mm) in diameter and 6" (150 mm) long. Shape the ends to a point and wrap the snake around a bamboo skewer. You have now made a coil bead, which can be baked on the skewer (see page 17).

MAKING A COILED COIL BEAD

To make a coiled coil bead, make a very long, thin extrusion and a shorter, thicker one. Wind the thin extrusion tightly around the thicker one, from one end to the other.

Wrap the coil around a bamboo skewer or metal knitting needle. After two or three turns, cut the coil and tuck the ends in neatly.

MAKING A DONUT BEAD

To make a donut bead, start by making a coil bead. Using a tissue blade, cut along the full length of the wrapped clay.

Remove the cut pieces from the skewer and separate them. Make them into round donut shapes by putting the ends together and smoothing the join. The beads can now be baked on polyester fiberfill (see page 17).

CHAIN LINK

Chain links lack thread holes, so strictly speaking they are not beads. They are, however, delightfully easy to make. For a very long chain, bake it in several sections and then join the sections up on the last baking.

TOOLS & MATERIALS

- Polymer clay in a variety of colors
- Large pen or similar
- Tissue blade
- Polymer clay repelling medium
- Polyester fiberfill

MAKING A CHAIN

Roll thin strings (see page 18) from different colored polymer clays. Roll and twist the thin strings together to make a randomly striped snake (see page 18). Wrap the snake around a thick pen then, using a tissue blade, cut individual loops from around the pen to make single open chain links.

Assemble the links into a chain. Start by joining the ends of one link, then adding another open link, and joining the ends of the new link. To stop the links from sticking to each other during assembly and baking, apply a coat of repelling medium to a link before adding another. When you have completed the chain, bake it on a piece of fiberfill (see page 17).

▶ **SEE ALSO** ▶ *Using a pasta machine, page 14* ▶ *Making logs and sheets, page 18* ▶ *Cutting and slicing, page 28*

A necklace of black-and-white striped twist stick beads threaded with red spacer beads.

Plain, striped, and flat corkscrew beads.

Three pastel-colored twist stick beads.

CORKSCREW

Corkscrew beads are delightfully simple. Their open shapes have a lighter feel than more tightly wound coil beads.

TOOLS & MATERIALS
- Polymer clay—either a plain color or make a multicolored snake
- Wooden dowel or metal knitting needle
- Needle tool
- Polyester fiberfill

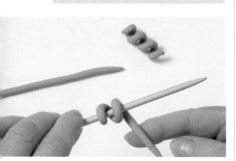

MAKING A CORKSCREW

Roll a snake from polymer clay about ¼" (6 mm) thick and 5" (125 mm) long. Roll the ends of the snake to make them pointed. Wrap the whole snake around the dowel or knitting needle, leaving gaps between each rotation of the snake.

Make a hole through the end of the clay with a needle tool or form a little loop out of the clay at one end of the snake through which a cord can be threaded. Either bake the corkscrew beads on the dowel or knitting needle or remove them and bake on polyester fiberfill (see page 17).

TWIST STICK

This is another basic shape that lends itself well to experimentation with colors, mixes, and sizes.

TOOLS & MATERIALS
- Polymer clay
- Pasta machine
- Tissue blade
- Ruler
- Needle tool
- Straight wire for baking

MAKING A TWIST STICK

Roll the clay into sheets on the thickest setting of a pasta machine. Stack the sheets to make a 1 x 2" (25 x 50 mm) wide block that is ⅜" (10 mm) high. Using a tissue blade and a ruler, cut slices the same width as the height of the stack.

With a needle tool, pierce the block through its full length. Hold one end steady and, with the other hand, gently twist the clay 90°.

Bake the beads lying flat or on a straight wire (see page 17).

TWISTED SPIRAL

The Twisted Spiral is a variation on the coil bead—it works best with contrasting colors.

Rolled snakes in contrasting colors.

Twist the two snakes together.

MAKING A STRIPED SNAKE

Roll the white clay into a snake 5" (125 mm) long. Roll the purple clay into a snake the same size. Put the two snakes next to each other and using both hands, roll them together into another snake. Roll your hands in opposite directions and twist the snake to make the stripes. Continue rolling and twisting until the stripes are as fine as you want, then begin to roll and push your hands toward the center of the clay snake. This will form a shaped snake with a thick center and tapered ends. To make finer stripes, use just your fingertips to twist the ends more.

Wrap the shaped snake around a bamboo skewer, tucking in the ends.

TOOLS & MATERIALS
- Polymer clay—equal amounts of white and purple
- Bamboo skewer

Twist and taper the ends.

Wrap the twisted clay around a skewer.

Bake the beads (see page 17) on the skewer, supporting it at each end. If the cooled baked beads are difficult to remove from the skewer, pop it back in the oven to slightly rewarm the clay.

Plain blue tube beads in different thicknesses with thread-holes through their lengths.

A multistranded necklace of evenly-striped black-and-white tube beads.

Two Nautilus beads; one using a striped clay, the other made from a Skinner blend.

TUBE

To make uniform rolled tube beads with a ready-made threading hole, try this technique of rolling with a piece of wire and a glass sheet. Be sure to blunt the edges of the glass first (see page 14).

TOOLS & MATERIALS

- Polymer clay
- Straight piece of wire about 5" (125 mm) long
- Two pieces of ¼" (6 mm) wooden dowel or
- knitting needles
- Small piece of glass
- Ruler
- Tissue blade or craft knife

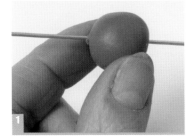

ROLLING THE BEAD

Roll a ¾" (18 mm) ball of clay in your hands. Pierce the ball through the center with straight wire, running the wire right through the ball. Roll the clay backward and forward into a log, using your hands to spread the clay along the wire. Stop when the log is about 3" (75 mm) long and ⅜" (10 mm) thick. If the clay loosens around the wire, press it back along the whole length of the wire and roll again.

MAKING EQUAL-SIZE BEADS

To make all the beads the same thickness, put a ¼" (6 mm) dowel or knitting needle at each end of the wire and place the piece of glass on top of the log. Holding the glass with both hands, move the glass backward and forward over the clay log to extend the clay farther along the wire, until the log is the same thickness as the dowel or knitting needles.

BAKING THE BEADS

While the clay is still on the wire, measure and mark the log into equal portions, then cut the portions with a tissue blade. Remove the beads and bake (see page 17). Or bake the beads on the wire and, when cool, remove the wire and snap the beads apart.

To make evenly striped tube beads, build a layered stack with contrasting colors 2" (50 mm) wide and ½" (12 mm) thick. Cut a ½" (12 mm) slice from the stack. Push a wire through the center and pinch to form a log.

Roll the log, letting the clay twist.

Continue to roll and twist until the clay is about 5" (125 mm) long.

Mark the clay into equal portions and cut with a craft knife or tissue blade.

NAUTILUS

This bead shape is inspired by the elegant spiral found in the shell form of the nautilus—an ancient sea creature known as a "living fossil."

TOOLS & MATERIALS

- Polymer clay
- Small piece of glass
- Needle tool
- Polyester fiberfill

ROLLING A CONE

Roll the clay into balls ¾" (18 mm) in diameter. Hold a piece of glass at an angle to the work surface and place a ball of clay underneath it. Move the glass backward and forward several times across the ball to shape it into a cone about 2½" (62 mm) long.

FINISHING THE BEAD

Hold the wide end of the shape and carefully roll the pointed end into a spiral, using your index finger to push the clay into the nautilus shape. Make a thread hole with the needle tool through any part of the bead, then bake the beads on a piece of fiberfill (see page 17).

▶ SEE ALSO   ▶ Using a pasta machine, page 14   ▶ Making logs and sheets, page 18

A necklace of pastel-colored macaroni beads joined with short lengths of rubber cord.

Macaroni beads made from a random striped snake.

MACARONI

Macaroni beads are made from snakes of clay of the same thickness. Join them together with short lengths of cord to create the illusion of a single threaded necklace.

TOOLS & MATERIALS
- Polymer clay
- Two pieces of ¼" (6 mm) wooden dowel or knitting needles
- Small piece of glass
- Ruler
- Tissue blade
- Polyester fiberfill
- Drill and drill bit
- Rubber cord
- Superglue

ROLLING OUT THE BEAD

Roll a log to about ⅜" (10 mm) diameter—roll it backward and forward on the work surface with your hands while at the same time rolling toward the ends of the log to lengthen it.

To make all the beads the same thickness, put a ¼" (6 mm) dowel or knitting needle at each end of the clay log and place a piece of glass over the top. Holding the glass with both hands, move the glass backward and forward over the clay log until the clay is the same thickness as the knitting needles.

Using the ruler, mark out 1½" (37 mm) lengths, then cut the portions using a tissue blade.

ADDING THE CORD

Using your thumb and index finger, bend the clay into a macaroni shape. Bake the pieces supported on polyester fiberfill (see page 17).

After baking, drill about ¼" (6 mm) into the bead ends with a drill bit the same size as the rubber cord to be used. Cut the rubber cord into ¾" (18 mm) pieces, apply a small amount of superglue to one end of the cord, and insert the glued cord into the drilled hole. Allow the glue to harden before gluing the other end of the rubber cord into the next macaroni bead.

> ▶ Tip
> ▶ Before baking the macaroni beads, make a small indentation in the center of both ends of each bead to help drilling the holes for the cord.

PLEATED BEAD

This is just one example of what you can make by simply folding and twisting a strip of polymer clay.

TOOLS & MATERIALS
- Polymer clay—black, gold mica, copper mica, and silver mica
- Pasta machine
- Tissue blade
- Brayer or roller
- Needle tool
- Paper for baking
- 400–800-grit wet and dry sandpapers (optional)
- Buffing cloth (optional)

ROLLING THE CLAYS

Roll out the black clay on a thin setting on the pasta machine. Make a Skinner blend (see page 22) with the gold, copper, and silver mica clays, using the full width of the pasta machine on its thickest setting. Using a tissue blade, cut off a 1½" (37 mm) wide strip across the Skinner blend and lay it on top of the black sheet.

Roll the clay sheets together with a brayer or roller to expel any trapped air pockets. Trim the edges of the black sheet using the tissue blade. Turn the piece over and place blended side down on another piece of thin black clay. Roll the clay again and trim the edges.

Pleated beads—one made from a strip of black-and-white layered clay and the other from a Skinner-blended clay sheet.

A folded black-and-white bead decorated with a pastel-colored striped snake and a necklace of beads in randomly striped black and white.

CUTTING AND PLEATING A STRIP

Use a tissue blade to cut a ¼" (6 mm) wide strip from the stacked clay.

Turn the strip on its edge and fold into loose, snakelike pleats (as illustrated).

BAKING AND FINISHING THE BEAD

Make a thread hole through the center of all the pleats with a needle tool. Lay the beads flat on a piece of paper and bake (see page 17). After baking, the edges of the beads can be wet-sanded and buffed to emphasize the shimmer effect of the mica particles in the clay.

FOLDED BEAD

Folded beads are based on early glass beads from Persia (Iran). There are different versions of folded beads, but here, a slice from a striped stack has been folded with two loops, forming very regular beads that are decorated with strings of twisted colored clays.

> **TOOLS & MATERIALS**
> - Polymer clay—white, black, and a selection of different colors
> - Pasta machine
> - Tissue blade
> - Needle tool
> - Polyester fiberfill

ROLLING A FOLDED BEAD

To make a slab of thin layers, roll out the white clay and the black clay on a thick setting on a pasta machine. Place the sheets together and roll through again without altering the setting. Halve and stack and roll through again. Cut this sheet into four pieces and then stack the pieces to make a slab ½ x 4" (12 x 100 mm) high. Using a tissue blade, cut a ½" (12 mm) slice from the stack to make a square log 4" (100 mm) long. Pinch along the log with your fingertips to slightly round the edges. Trim the ends using a tissue blade and join the ends together neatly, matching the stripes.

Shape the clay into an oval. Place a finger on either side of the clay and roll the clay inward from the sides until the underside of the clay stack is on top.

Push the long sides of the oval together until they meet, then fold the clay back along its length so the two ends meet. Neaten the loops using your fingers.

ADDING A STRIPED SNAKE

Twist the multicolored clays into a striped snake. Roll the ends out to make a point at each end. Check that the snake is long enough to fit into the groove around the bead, then carefully insert it into the groove. Make a second snake and fit it into the other groove. Make a thread hole with the needle tool along the length of the bead and through the centers of both twisted snakes. Bake the bead lying flat on polyester fiberfill (see page 17).

▶ **SEE ALSO** ▶ *Making logs and sheets, page 18* ▶ *Skinner blends, page 22*

A necklace of foxglove trumpet-shaped beads.

Two trumpet-flower beads made with textured, translucent clay patinated with iridescent paints.

TRUMPET

This bead is inspired by the foxglove flower. The flower petal is made from a two-tone sheet, which is dark pink on one side and pale pink on the other side. The spotted cane is a bull's eye cane (see page 31), which has been reduced, cut, and stacked several times.

TOOLS & MATERIALS
- Polymer clay—maroon, white, black, orange, yellow, and green
- Pasta machine
- Tissue blade
- Brayer or roller
- 1½" (30mm) round
- cookie cutter
- Star cookie cutter
- Needle tool
- Piece of wire or thin knitting needle
- Polyester fiberfill

1 MAKING THE PETAL SHEETS

Make the dark petal blend by mixing one part of maroon clay to one part of white clay. Make the pale petal blend by mixing 12 parts of white clay with a speck of maroon clay.

Roll the two colored clays into medium thick sheets using a pasta machine. Cut one of the sheets into a rectangle using a tissue blade, place it on the other colored sheet, and trim the edges. Roll the two sheets together through the pasta machine on the thickest setting. Reduce the setting and roll again. Do this two more times until the clay is a medium thickness. Put to one side.

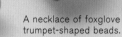

MAKING THE INNER SPOTTED CANE

Roll some black clay into a log 3–4" (75–100 mm) long and ½" (12 mm) in diameter. Using a pasta machine, roll out a sheet of white clay on the thickest setting. Wrap two layers of the white sheet around the black log, butting the joins and trimming off any excess clay. Using your hands, roll out the log to reduce it to about ½" (12 mm) in diameter and about 12" (300 mm) in length. Cut the log into four pieces, stack together, and roll out again. Cut into seven pieces and stack together. Roll out and again, cut into seven pieces and stack together.

SLICING THE CANE

At this stage, don't roll the cane but leave the shape of the logs around the outside. Using a tissue blade, cut a thin slice from the spotted cane.

4 APPLYING THE SLICE

Place the slice of spotted cane on either the dark or the pale side of the two-colored sheet and use the roller or brayer to gently roll the slice into the clay until it is smooth. Using a round cookie cutter, cut out a circle around the slice.

5 CREATING THE STAMENS

Roll the orange clay into a thin string, cut off tiny pieces, and roll each piece into a ball. Roll the yellow clay into a thin string and cut into 1–2" (25–50 mm) lengths. Add an orange ball to the end of each of the yellow pieces and roll together to join.

Place a pair of stamens on one of the circle cut-outs and curl the sides of the circle around to form the flower.

MAKING THE SEPAL

Roll out the green clay on a thin setting of the pasta machine. Cut out star shapes with the cookie cutter and make a thread hole in each using a needle tool. Push wire or a thin knitting needle through the flower and thread on one of the green pieces. Smooth it down onto the flower. Bake the flowers resting on polyester fiberfill (see page 17).

6

A group of beads made in an oval bead roller, some reshaped into bun or cube beads.

A necklace of rainbow-colored beads rolled in different size round bead rollers.

BEAD ROLLERS

A bead roller is a wonderful tool for consistently making perfectly shaped beads in a variety of sizes and shapes. Here, an oval bead roller has been used.

TOOLS & MATERIALS

- Polymer clay— black, white, and red
- Tissue blade
- Pasta machine
- ½" (12 mm) round cookie cutter
- Oval bead roller
- Needle tool

USING A BEAD ROLLER

Roll out black and white balls of clay using your hands (follow the manufacturer's instructions for the amount of clay required for the bead roller). Cut the black and white balls in half using a tissue blade.

Roll out a thin sheet of red clay using a pasta machine and cut out a few disk shapes with a cookie cutter. Put a red disk between half a black and half a white ball. Cut the ball in half so the red disk is cut in half, flip 180°, and rejoin so the black and white clays alternate and the red disk appears whole again. Gently press the four quarters together.

Place the bead in the middle of the base of the bead roller with the axis of the bead horizontal to the bed of the bead roller. Put the top part of the bead roller onto the base and slide backward and forward a few times to roll the bead into an oval shape.

To make the stripes in the bead, reposition the bead at one end of the channel, replace the lid, and slide it to the other end. Remove the lid and put the bead back at the beginning of the channel without turning it. Replace the lid and slide it to the other end again.

Continue to move the bead back to the beginning, slide the lid over it, and gradually the lines on the bead will move around the bead, making an interesting striped oval bead. Make a thread hole using a needle tool, then bake (see page 17).

FOIL CORE BEAD

Although baked polymer clay is lighter than most natural bead materials, large beads in a necklace can be heavy to wear. To avoid this, try making a bead core from crushed aluminum foil.

TOOLS & MATERIALS

- Aluminum foil
- Polymer clay
- Pasta machine
- Craft knife
- Scissors
- Needle tool

MAKING A FOIL BALL

Scrunch some aluminum foil into a tight ¾" (18 mm) diameter ball.

MAKING THE OUTER LAYER

Roll out the clay into a sheet on the thickest setting of the pasta machine.

Cut out a 2–3" (50–75 mm) circle with a craft knife. Place the foil ball in the center of the clay circle and bring the clay up around the foil ball. Using your fingertips, pinch the excess clay to form tucks or pleats around the core.

TRIMMING AWAY EXCESS CLAY

Press the clay onto the foil and cut off the excess clay with a pair of scissors. Use your fingers to smooth the joins.

FINISHING THE BEAD

Roll the ball in the palms of your hands to form it into a sphere. Pierce the bead with a needle tool to make the thread hole (a sharp needle tool should go through the bead and foil). Roll the bead again if it has become distorted. You can decorate the beads before or after baking (see page 17).

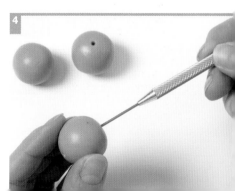

A necklace of jigsaw beads sanded to create true cube shapes, with threadholes made diagonally from one point of the cube to the other.

DRILLING, SANDING, POLISHING, &VARNISHING

ONCE YOU HAVE MADE YOUR BEADS you will want to prepare them for making into a finished piece. The techniques shown here produce fine polymer dust. Always wear eye protection and wear a mask to avoid breathing in any dust.

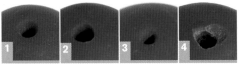

1 A smooth hole made in the raw clay using a pointed tool.
2 A clean drilled hole. Drilling from both ends keeps the baked clay from shelling.
3 A hole made with a small drill bit. Increasing the drill bit size gradually prevents the clay "shelling."
4 A badly drilled bead hole where the exit has "shelled."

DRILLING

You need to think about the size of thread or cord that the beads will be threaded onto and whether to make the hole before or after baking. It is usually easier to make the thread-hole with a needle tool before baking. However, pushing a large needle through soft clay may distort the bead. Drill larger holes, for threading with a leather thong or rubber cord, after baking.

> ▶ **Tip**
> ▶ Hold the drill vertically to the work surface. When you use the largest drill bit, drill from both ends of the thread hole to prevent any "shelling" around the exit hole.

DRILLING A HOLE

Before you bake the clay, make a small needle hole or dimple in the soft clay, then, after baking, drill out the hole using an electric craft tool. Begin with a small drill bit of ⅛" (3 mm) or less, and gradually increase the drill bit size until the hole is large enough.

A dimple made in soft clay, ready for drilling.

SANDING

The natural matt finish of baked polymer clay is attractive and also unusual, as many bead materials are shiny. However, baked polymer clay can also be sanded, polished, or varnished to look shiny, and varnishing is more effective if the beads are presanded.

WET-SANDING

Sand polymer clay with wet sandpaper. Use waterproof sandpaper of 400-, 600-, and 800-grit sizes (you can use up to 1200 but 800 is usually high enough). Begin with the coarser grade, working to the finest.

To avoid breathing dust, hold the bead under running water or keep dipping it in water with a drop of liquid soap or detergent added. Change the water after each grade of paper.

A necklace
of round black
beads inlaid with
slices of an extruded
cane and polished to a high
shine using a buffing wheel.

HAND POLISHING

If you have a few small beads, or prefer a less glossy finish, you can buff them by hand.

BUFFING WITH CLOTH

Baked clay beads can be buffed by hand with paper towels, cotton cloth, or a piece of denim—this produces a satin finish.

Sanding your bead first will result in a more shiny polish.

MACHINE POLISHING

An electric craft tool with a cotton mop-head, or muslin-wheel attachment is ideal for polishing a few beads. Use an electric buffing machine for larger quantities and a higher shine.

USING A BUFFING MACHINE

When using a buffing machine, tie back long hair, and secure loose clothing. Hold the bead at the underside of the buffing wheel (4–5 o'clock) as it rotates toward you at a high speed. Try to keep the bead moving and don't press it against the buffer or this can begin to heat the surface of the bead. Be careful, as the buffing wheel may "snatch" the bead and throw it away from you. Place an open cardboard box behind the buffing wheel to catch any beads that are snatched from your hands.

Don't use polishing compound as particles of polish may imbed into the bead's surface and spoil the finished look.

VARNISHING

While sanding and polishing give a professional finish to beads, it may be more practical to simply varnish, or sand and varnish them, especially if you do not have space for a polishing machine.

Use water-based acrylic floor varnish to give a glossy finish. You can also dilute a water-based varnish with a small amount of water to give the bead a satin finish.

Excluding polymer-clay manufacturers' own-brand varnishes, solvent-based varnishes and lacquers, including clear nail polish, are not advisable as they often react with baked clay and either never dry completely or become sticky after a few weeks. Always test solvent-based products on a sample bead first.

Plain baked bead   Matt varnish   Clear varnish   Gloss varnish

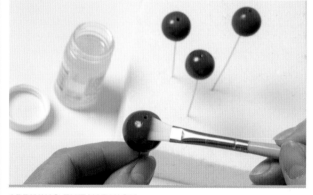

APPLYING THE VARNISH

Whichever varnish you choose, use a short stiff wire to hold the bead while you varnish it. Hold the wire and apply a coat of varnish with a paintbrush. Support each wire in a block of polystyrene while the varnish dries.

None   Buffed by hand   Buffed by machine

▶ **SEE ALSO** ▶ Findings and threads, page 104

Several Rope Twist beads baked and while hot, held slightly curved.

A necklace of beads that are the cut slices from a black-and-white clay extrusion, strung with black bugle beads.

Miniature extruded clay slices, shown at actual size.

EXTRUSIONS

EXTRUDER TOOLS ARE VERY USEFUL for the polymer clay artist. You can purchase a simple one from a craft store. They come with a variety of dies (plates) to make extrusions of different cross sections. There are many ways of using extruded clay. It can be wrapped around a shape such as a ball of clay, wound around a skewer as in the coiled beads, (see page 41), or imitate silver wire (see page 90). A range of different effects can be made depending on how you load the barrel of the tool with different colors and layers.

To make the process easier, make sure that the clay is well conditioned (see page 16) and softened (some brands of clay are easier to extrude than others).

EXTRUDING CLAY

Load the tool barrel from either end. It is often easier to load small quantities of clay from the die end by unscrewing the collar and removing the die plate.

Use logs, pellets, or stacks of clay made up from disks cut using a cookie cutter. When loading two or more colors, it is better to fill the barrel only halfway with 1¼" (30 mm) lengths as later extrusions from a mixed barrel can become muddy.

After use, take the extruder gun apart and clean with paper towels, hand fresheners (wet-wipes), or makeup removal pads.

CONCENTRIC BEADS

Loading layers of different-colored clay into the extruder tool surprisingly results in a polymer clay extrusion containing concentric circles. These are revealed with subtle variations when the extruded clay is cut into slices. This is the same technique as used for the extruded malachite (see page 93).

> ▶ **Tip**
> ▶ Make short stacks as the red will only appear on the outside of the first part of the extrusion.

MAKING THE DISKS

Roll the black, red, and white clays into medium thick sheets using a pasta machine. Cut out disks from each colored sheet using the cookie cutter. Stack the disks, starting with a red disk, and followed by alternate black and white disks. Make each stack about 1¼" (30 mm) high. Compress one of the stacks and fit it into the front of the barrel of the extruder tool.

TOOLS & MATERIALS
CONCENTRIC BEADS
- Polymer clay—black, white, and red
- Pasta machine
- ½" (12 mm) round cookie cutter
- Extruder tool with ⅜" (9 mm) die
- Craft knife
- Needle tool
- Piece of paper for baking

ROPE TWIST BEADS
- Polymer clay in various colors
- 1¼" (30 mm) round cookie cutter
- Extruder tool with small die
- Tissue blade
- Polyester fiberfill

WRAPPED BEADS
- Polymer clay in various colors
- Extruder tool with small die
- Needle tool
- Clay shaper

THE EXTRUSION TOOL

The extrusion tool with different dies (plates) and different shapes of extruded clay. There are several types of extruder tools available.

> **Tip**
> ▶ In winter, keep the extruder barrel on top of a radiator so it is always warm and ready for use.

An extruded string of several colors meanders in curves and twirls around a colored ball.

A necklace of wrapped beads and small silver beads.

ROPE TWIST BEADS

Extruded clay is twisted so that it resembles rope. The sides are then sliced to reveal the layers within.

EXTRUDING THE CLAY

Extrude the clay and cut the log into ⅛" (3 mm) slices using a craft knife. Make a thread hole with the needle tool through each bead, from edge to edge. Bake the beads lying flat on a piece of paper (see page 17). Clean the extruder tool with paper towels after each extrusion.

EXTRUDING THE CLAY

Roll each colored clay into medium-thick sheets using a pasta machine. Using the cookie cutter, cut disks from each sheet and stack into 1¼" (30 mm) piles starting with a color and alternating colored and white disks. Compact each clay stack so it fits into the extruder barrel. Insert the plunger and extrude the clay. Clean the tool with paper towels to be ready for reloading.

MAKING A TWISTED ROPE

Hold the extruded clay at each end and twist it gently to form a rope. Cut the rope into equal lengths using a tissue blade. Hold one and carefully slice into the clay with the tissue blade to reveal the layers within the clay. It is safer to cut away from your hand than toward it. Make the thread hole along the length of the bead with a needle tool. Bake on polyester fiberfill (see page 17).

WRAPPED BEADS

Use an extrusion to wrap a core of scrap clay. Round beads are shown here, but you could experiment with other shapes.

MAKING A LOG

Make a log with a random mix of pieces of each colored clay and fit it into the barrel of the extruder tool.

EXTRUDING THE CLAY

Fit the plunger into the extruder tool and extrude the clay. Notice how the color changes along the length of the extruded clay.

WRAPPING AROUND THE BEAD

Roll a ¾" (18 mm) ball of scrap clay and pierce a hole through the center with a needle tool. Working with the bead on the needle tool, coil a small loop of extruded clay and place it around the needle and over the hole. Rotate the needle tool and bead to wrap the extruded clay around the ball, laying on the same color or twisting the extruded clay so a different color shows on each rotation.

Turn the needle tool to the other end of the bead and continue wrapping the clay around the bead. Remove the needle tool and use a pointed clay shaper to neaten the clay at the thread holes and bake the beads lying on polyester fiberfill (see page 17).

▶ **SEE ALSO** ▶ Conditioning, page 16 ▶ Making logs and sheets, page 18 ▶ Malachite, page 92

A necklace of dichroic beads threaded in groups of three.

Lengths of dark scrap clay tied into knots, decorated with a metallic finish.

FOILS, POWDERS, AND GLITTERS

THERE ARE SEVERAL WAYS OF ADDING SPARKLE to polymer clay.

Foils are plastic sheets with a thin colored or metallic coating that can be transferred, by pressure or heat, to prepared surfaces, including baked and unbaked polymer clay.

Metal leaf comes in very thin square sheets separated by sheets of tissue paper. There is no backing to metal leaf, and either side of the leaf adheres readily to raw clay or varnished baked clay. The clay should be sealed afterward with varnish.

Metallic powders can be used on the surface of the clay or mixed into translucent clay. They must be sealed so they don't rub off with wear. Wear a mask when working with metallic powders.

Glitter is made up of coarse powder or finely chopped metal foils that can be sprinkled onto varnished surfaces or mixed with translucent clays.

Foils can be used on polymer clay with exciting glittery effects. Mark up the surface of a baked bead with a "pen" filled with adhesive. When the adhesive is nearly dry, decorate with the foils.

DICHROIC BEADS

Sheets of metallic silver leaf are applied to polymer clay. The clay is then stretched so the foil cracks. You can also apply splashes of paint, which will crackle with the foil and produce random effects. The beads are finished by applying water-based floor polish, which makes the surface appear like dichroic glass (taking on two or more colors).

STACKING THE SHEETS

Roll out the black clay and scrap clay separately, into sheets on the thickest setting of the pasta machine. Cut both sheets to the same size using a tissue blade and stack together, with the black on top, to make a double-thickness sheet.

TOOLS & MATERIALS
DICHROIC BEADS
- Black polymer clay
- Dark scrap polymer clay
- Pasta machine
- Tissue blade
- Silver metal leaf
- Acrylic-/spirit-based paints
- Cotton swabs or similar
- Wax/greaseproof paper
- Roller or brayer
- ¾" (18 mm) square cookie cutter
- Dust mask
- Paintbrush
- Gold powder
- Needle tool
- Piece of paper, for baking
- Water-based acrylic floor polish
- Ranger's Poly-Glaze

SPARKLING BLACK BEADS
- Polymer clay—black and argent
- Needle tool
- Wire
- Foil adhesive pen and foils
- Knitting needle
- Polystyrene block
- Water-based acrylic floor polish

ADDING SILVER LEAF

Cover the black clay with a sheet of silver leaf and smooth the leaf flat onto the clay. It is easier to place the clay onto the silver leaf rather than lifting the silver leaf onto the clay. Paint the silver leaf in a random pattern with the paints using a cotton swab or your finger and leave to dry.

BAKING THE BEADS

Using the needle tool, make a thread hole from the inside corner of the cut-out square across the bead to exit at the opposite corner. Bake the pieces lying flat on a piece of paper (see page 17).

A group of beads covered in "starbursts" of decorative foils.

Cube beads of translucent clay mixed with colored glitters and threaded from point to point.

ROLLING THE SHEET

When the painted surface is completely dry, place between two sheets of wax paper. Using the roller or brayer, roll the clay from the center of the sheet toward the edges while applying pressure to crackle the foil. When the sheet is thin enough, roll the sheet through the pasta machine. This will lengthen the clay sheet and crackle the silver foil further.

LAYERING THE DECORATIVE CLAY

Roll out a sheet of dark scrap clay on a medium to thick setting on the pasta machine. Cut the decorative sheet in half and place one half of the decorative sheet face up on top of the scrap clay sheet. Trim the edges with a tissue blade. Lay the other half of the decorative sheet on the other side of the scrap clay. Smooth the layers with a roller or brayer to expel any trapped air.

CUTTING OUT SHAPES

Place the clay sheet on the work surface. Using a square cookie cutter, cut out pieces from the most interesting parts of the painted sheet. Check the other side of the sheet before cutting out the pieces to ensure you are cutting from the best area. Use a corner of the square cookie cutter to cut out a corner from each cut-out square.

APPLYING GOLD POWDER

Put on a mask. With a small paintbrush, carefully "paint" gold powder onto all the undecorated edges of the cut-out pieces.

VARNISHING THE BEADS

Leave to cool, then apply two coats of glaze to each decorative side of the bead, allowing the first coat to dry completely before applying the second. Paint the edges with acrylic polish to prevent the gold powder from rubbing off and to seal the glaze.

SPARKLING BLACK BEADS

Use a sparkling mix of clay and foil for these beads. Follow the manufacturer's instructions to apply the foil.

1 PREPARING THE BEADS

Mix together black and argent clay in equal proportions. Roll a ¾" (18 mm) ball of clay in your hands. With the needle tool make a thread hole, then bake (see page 17). When the bead is cool, place it on the needle tool or on a short stiff wire. Using the adhesive pen, apply a blob of adhesive to the ball.

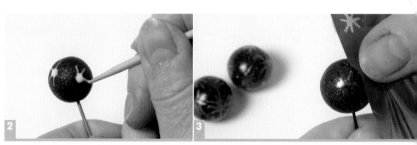

2 MAKING STAR SHAPES

Using a knitting needle, drag the adhesive into a star shape. Repeat, making several stars around the bead. Transfer the bead to a short wire, stand it in the polystyrene block, and leave the adhesive to "dry" for a few minutes. It will become transparent but will still be sticky to the touch.

3 APPLYING THE FOIL

Apply the foil (with the colored side away from the ball) to the adhesive, press, and pull the foil away. The foil will stick to the adhesive. If some areas remain without color, place the foil on the adhesive again.

Apply a light coat of polish, then leave the bead to dry.

Rainbow-colored beads with appliqués of small slices from a Skinner blend jelly roll cane.

Beads decorated with "divot" slices and threaded with color-blended beads.

APPLIQUÉ

APPLIQUÉ IS AN EMBROIDERY TERM used to describe a piece of fabric stitched onto another piece of fabric. Similarly, simple decorative shapes of unbaked polymer clay, such as cookie cutter cut-outs or slices of cane, can easily be stuck onto other pieces of clay to create a bead with both texture and pattern. The shapes remain on the surface of the bead and are not rolled into the clay as with some "inlay" beads.

COOKIE CUTTER SHAPES

Use a tiny cookie cutter to make these delicate spotted beads.

MAKING THE SPOTTED BEADS

Mix each colored clay (except black) with an equal amount of white clay. Roll the clays through the pasta machine on a thin to medium setting. Cut out shapes with the cookie cutter. Roll the black clay into ½" (12 mm) diameter balls and make a thread hole through the center of each ball.

Place a ball onto the end of the needle tool and press cut-out pieces onto it, being careful not to distort the

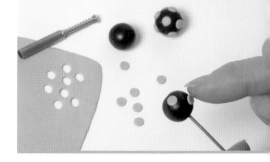

shape. Repeat for the other beads.

Place the beads on polyester fiberfill and bake (see page 17). Cool, then apply a finish of your choice.

TOOLS & MATERIALS

COOKIE CUTTER SHAPES
- Polymer clay—black, white, and several other colors
- Pasta machine
- Small round cookie cutter
- Needle tool
- Polyester fiberfill
- Water-based floor polish

CARVED DIVOTS
- Polymer clay—white and four different colors
- Pasta machine
- Tissue blade
- Roller or brayer
- U-shaped linoleum cutter
- Needle tool
- Craft knife
- Clay shaper or similar (optional)
- Polyester fiberfill
- Water-based floor polish

1

CARVED DIVOTS

Cut "divots" from a layered sheet using a sharp linoleum cutter.

MAKING THE SHEETS

Roll a medium-thick sheet of each clay using the pasta machine. Cut the sheets into 2 x 2" (50 x 50 mm) squares using a tissue blade and stack them, alternating colors with white. Compress the stack with a roller or brayer until it is ⅛" (3 mm) thick. Using the cutter, cut divots from both sides of the layered sheet. Lay the pieces on the work surface so the layers are visible.

2

FINISHING THE BEADS

Roll ¾" (18 mm) diameter balls of white clay and make a thread hole through the center with the needle tool. Place one of the balls on the needle tool and apply the cut-out pieces around the ball—use the point of a craft knife to pick up and apply the pieces. Carefully press the pieces onto the surface of the clay, but avoid flattening them or distorting the ball. Use a clay shaper to secure the edges of the pieces onto the ball.

Place the beads on polyester fiberfill and bake (see page 17). Leave to cool, then varnish.

Appliqué beads with multicolored "divots." Note that the base color of each bead is different.

Metallic cube beads textured with various impressed tools *(far right)*.

Leaf beads cut out and textured with a cookie cutter.

TEXTURING

UNBAKED POLYMER CLAY REGISTERS an impression of whatever is pressed into it, and all sorts of shapes and tools can be used to make textured beads. Try using texture sheets, lace, leaves, rubber stamps, paper clips, pen tops, scrunched aluminum foil, or coins.

TOOLS & MATERIALS
- ½" (12 mm) cube-bead core made from scrap clay (see right)
- Black polymer clay
- Tissue blade
- Needle tool
- Pasta machine
- Liquid polymer clay
- Texture sheet or other texture tool
- Water in a spray bottle
- Dust mask
- Gold pearl powdered pigment
- Paintbrush
- Polyester fiberfill
- Water-based floor polish

TEXTURED CUBES
A texture sheet is used to impress black clay cubes, which are then brushed with gold powder to emphasize the textural marks.

MAKING THE CUBE-CORE BEAD
To make the core, build a stack of 10–12 layers of thick sheets of scrap clay. Cut into ½" (12 mm) cubes with a tissue blade, then make a thread hole with a needle tool and bake (see page 17).

COVERING THE BEAD CORE
Roll out the black clay on a medium-thick setting on the pasta machine. Apply a very thin layer of liquid clay to the baked core to bond the clays, then place the core onto the clay sheet. Using a tissue blade, cut around the core, pressing the clay gently onto it.
Place the opposite side of the core down onto the clay sheet and cut around it. Continue to cover all the sides of the core in black clay. Redefine the thread hole.

> ▶ **Tip**
> ▶ Use a cutter that impresses a texture. This leaf-shaped cutter is effective when used with fall colors.

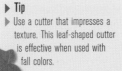

IMPRESSING THE BEAD
Lay the texture sheet on the work surface and spray with water to keep the clay from sticking to the sheet. Place the cube on the texture sheet and fold the other end of the sheet over the top of the cube. Press down evenly to impress the texture on both sides of the cube.
Lift the sheet, turn the cube, and impress another two sides. Repeat to impress the last pair of sides. Check the thread hole is still visible. Put the beads aside until the water has dried.

APPLYING GOLD POWDER
Wearing a dust mask, apply the gold pigment to the surface of the beads with a paintbrush or your fingertip. Place the beads on polyester fiberfill and bake (see page 17). Leave to cool, then apply a light coat of polish to seal the powder.

▶ **SEE ALSO**   ▶ Baking, page 17   ▶ Cutting and slicing, page 28

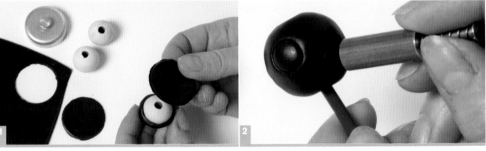

Two necklaces with "soft-into-soft" colored inlays.

INLAY

AN INLAID BEAD HAS A SMOOTH, decorated surface made up of two or more clays. You can also add inlaid "found objects," such as seeds, if they can withstand baking. To be sure objects can hold up to the baking, place one or two into your oven and run a baking cycle. If they survive, you can use them in your design.

SOFT-INTO-HARD INLAY

Also known as "backfilling," in this process you bake the surrounding clay first and then press in soft clay to fill the cut-out shapes.

COVERING THE BEAD CORE

Roll out a sheet of black clay on the thickest setting of the pasta machine. Cut two circles of black clay with the larger circular cookie cutter and place one on the base and one on top of the bead core. Wrap the clay around the core and smooth the join using your fingers. Reshape the ball by rolling it in the palms of your hands. If necessary, use a little liquid clay to help the outer clay stick to the bead core. Redefine the thread hole with a clay shaper, ensuring that the outer clay layer is pressed into the thread hole.

CUTTING OUT SHAPES

Support a ball on the handle of a paintbrush and cut shapes out of the black clay using the small cookie cutter. Cut out all the shapes before removing any of the clay so the clay does not become distorted. Remove the cut-out pieces and clean the cut-out shapes left in the clay. Place the beads on a piece of paper and bake (see page 17).

ADDING EXTRUDED SLICES

Make a multicolored extruded log following the method for Extruded Concentric beads (see page 51). Using the tissue blade, cut slices from the extruded clay log, a little thicker than the thickness of the black clay on the bead. Apply a little liquid clay to a cut-out area and place a slice of extruded clay into the space. Use your fingertip to press the slice into place. When all the spaces have been filled, bake the bead again (see page 17).

Leave the beads to cool, then wet-sand them. Buff the beads using a buffing wheel if you want a high gloss or use a piece of denim for a satin finish.

TOOLS & MATERIALS

SOFT-INTO-HARD INLAY	HARD-INTO-SOFT INLAY
● Black polymer clay	● Mother-of-pearl clay (see page 86)
● Multicolored extruded clay log (see page 50)	● Materials for making black beads (as for "Soft-Into-Hard" Inlay)
● Liquid polymer clay	● Liquid polymer clay
● Pasta machine	● Pasta machine
● 1" (25 mm) round cookie cutter	● Small flower-shaped cookie cutter
● ⅝" (15 mm) diameter baked bead core of pale scrap clay (with thread hole)	● Handle of paintbrush
	● Polyester fiberfill
● Clay shaper or similar	● 400–800-grit waterproof sandpapers
● Handle of paintbrush or similar	● Piece of denim or buffing wheel (optional)
● ⅜" (9 mm) round cookie cutter	
● Piece of paper for baking	SOFT-INTO-SOFT INLAY
● Tissue blade	● Polymer clay—black and white
● 400–800-grit waterproof sandpapers	● Knitting needles
● Piece of denim or buffing wheel (optional)	● Piece of glass
	● Needle tool
	● Paper bead rest

A necklace inlaid with mother-of-pearl flowers, using the "hard-into-soft" method.

Two disk beads decorated with inlays of faux abalone (see page 84).

HARD-INTO-SOFT INLAY

The shapes of the inlaid pieces stay unchanged using this technique.

MOTHER-OF-PEARL FLOWERS

Follow the instructions for making a sheet of mother-of-pearl clay (see page 86). Roll out the sheet on the thickest setting of the pasta machine. Using the flower-shaped cookie cutter, cut out flower shapes. Place the shapes flat on a piece of paper and bake (see page 17).

COVERING THE BEAD CORE

Make a black bead using the same method as for "Soft-Into-Hard Inlay" on the opposite page.

CUTTING OUT FLOWER SHAPES

Support a bead on the handle of a paintbrush. Cut shapes out of the black clay using the flower-shaped cookie cutter. Cut out all the flower shapes before removing any of the clay so the clay does not become distorted.

Remove the black flowers and clean the cut-out shapes left in the clay. The pale core helps to show when the cut-out shape is clean of clay bits.

APPLYING THE FLOWERS

Apply a spot of liquid clay to one of the holes on the bead and press a baked mother-of-pearl flower into the space. Repeat for all the flowers, then gently roll the ball to embed the inlays and ensure there are no gaps.

Place the beads on polyester fiberfill and bake (see page 17). Leave to cool, then wet-sand. Polish with a cloth or buffing wheel to enhance the mother-of-pearl effect.

SOFT-INTO-SOFT INLAY

This method of inlay takes advantage of the inevitable distortion that occurs when clay shapes are pressed together.

MAKING A LOG

Roll a ½" (12 mm) diameter ball of black clay into a small log using your fingertips.

APPLYING THE INLAID BALLS

Roll ⅛" (3 mm) diameter balls of white clay and position five or six balls around the middle of the black log. Gently press them onto the surface.

ROLLING OUT THE INLAID LOG

Place a knitting needle at each end of the clay log and lay a piece of glass on top. Move the glass backward and forward along the knitting needles to roll out the log and press the dots of white clay into the black clay.

BAKING THE BEAD

Press in both ends of the log to neaten them. Make a thread hole along the center of the tube bead with the needle tool. Place the beads on a paper bead rest to keep them straight, then bake (see page 17).

▶ **SEE ALSO** ▶ Baking, page 17 ▶ Drilling, page 48 ▶ Extrusions, page 50 ▶ Mother-of-pearl, page 88

A necklace of beads made from the leftover ends of canes.

Gold-and-black Rorschach beads.

RORSCHACH

"RORSCHACH" REFERS TO THE PSYCHOLOGICAL tests based on the interpretation of random ink blots, which have been popular since the 1930s. These mirror-image designs continue to be fascinating and unpredictable.

The beads made are really a double Rorschach. They have also been called "inside-out-beads," as the insides of the beads are literally turned to the outside; and "Natasha beads," after Natasha Flechsig who applied the technique to polymer clay.

Rorschach is used to surprising effect when you clump together leftover ends of canes, form them into a square shape, then cut them in half to reveal the mirror image. Each bead will turn out differently, and to make two beads the same is quite difficult. You need to follow a disciplined system to get a string of almost identical beads. You can experiment by introducing more colors or starting with a different cane. Experimenting will often make more scrap clay, ideal for the individual randomly patterned beads.

TOOLS & MATERIALS
- Polymer clay—black and white
- Roller or pasta machine
- Tissue blade
- Brayer or acrylic roller
- Needle tool
- Piece of paper for baking

MAKING THE CLAY SHEETS

Roll sheets of black and white clay using a roller or on a medium setting on a pasta machine. Using a tissue blade, cut the white sheet into a square 4½ x 4½" (115 mm x 115 mm) and carefully place it on top of the black sheet. Trim the edges of the black sheet with the tissue blade so that it is the same size as the white sheet. Roll to expel trapped air. Cut the sheet in half, across the width, using the tissue blade, and put half to one side to use for more beads later.

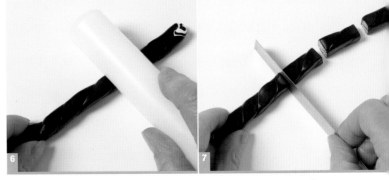

SQUARING UP THE LOG

Use a roller or brayer to flatten one side of the twisted log. Turn the log onto another side and roll to flatten the second side. Keep turning and rolling to make a square log.

FORMING THE BEADS

Cut the square log into equal-size bead portions with the tissue blade.

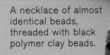

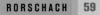

A necklace of almost identical beads, threaded with black polymer clay beads.

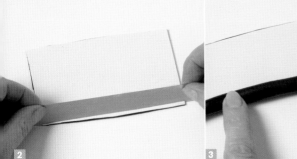

CUTTING THE CLAY

With the tissue blade held at an angle, cut the edge of the white sheet at an angle to expose the edge of the black sheet. Turn the clay 180° and repeat for the opposite edge.

MAKING A ROLL

Roll the clay up carefully to form a "jelly roll."

LENGTHENING THE ROLL

Use your fingertips to roll the jelly roll out to twice its original length. Cut in half and place the two rolls side by side. Roll the halves together so they combine to form a log.

TWISTING THE LOG

Twist the log by rolling each hand in the opposite directions. The log will tend to get longer as you do this.

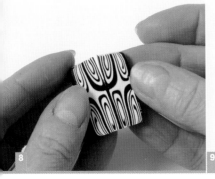

THE MIRROR IMAGE

Cut a portion in half along its length. Open the halves to reveal the mirror image. Align two of the cut edges of the pattern and carefully push together; avoid distorting the pattern.

HALVING AGAIN

Place the mirror image side of the bead face down and cut each half in two.

MORE MIRROR IMAGES

Turn over and open up the cuts to reveal more mirror images, and turn the corners back on themselves to make the bead. With a tissue blade cut the ends of the bead to square them up. Make a thread hole, bake on fiberfill, and finish the bead as desired.

▶ **Tip**
▶ When squaring the ends of the bead, do not just cut from the top down as this will tend to distort the bead. Instead, hold the blade slightly tilted away from the bead and cut the lower edge. Roll the bead onto its side and cut the next edge. Keep turning the bead and cutting until all four edges have been cut. Now repeat these four cuts for the other end of the bead.

▶ **SEE ALSO** ▶ *Using a pasta machine, page 14* ▶ *Making logs and sheets, page 18* ▶ *Mica-shift technique, page 66*

Cube beads with a flower transfer picture on four sides and a layered square bead of pink and white clay with a flower transfer on the front and back.

TRANSFERS

THERE ARE MANY COMMERCIAL PRODUCTS that can be used to transfer printed images onto polymer clay beads. This method uses an inkjet printer and transfer paper. Follow the manufacturer's instructions but also be prepared to experiment. Think about the style and size of images you want on your beads and remember that the printed image will be reversed on the finished bead.

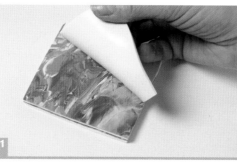

STACKING THE CLAY

Roll the white clay into sheets on the thickest setting of the pasta machine. Chop up the colored clays using a tissue blade, roll into a ball, then roll into very thin sheets using the pasta machine. (You could use a single color if you'd prefer.)

Make a stack, with white sheets on the top and bottom and alternating colored and white sheets in the middle. Smooth the layers with a roller or brayer to expel any air pockets.

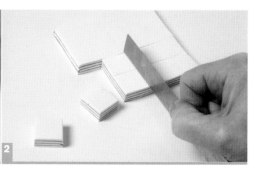

MAKING THE THREAD HOLE

Using a tissue blade, cut the stack into ¾" (18 mm) squares. Make a thread hole horizontally through the bead with the needle tool.

TOOLS & MATERIALS

- Polymer clay—white, and a mix of colors for the layered stack
- Pasta machine
- Tissue blade
- Roller or brayer
- Needle tool
- Image for scanning
- Scanner
- T-shirt transfer paper
- Inkjet printer
- Knitting needle or similar
- Tile or piece of glass
- Timer
- 800-grit wet and dry sandpaper
- Water-based acrylic floor polish

APPLYING THE PRINT

Scan the image you have chosen into your computer. Print it at the required size onto a piece of T-shirt transfer paper using an inkjet printer. Cut the printed sheet into squares that will fit onto the clay squares, and place face down on the clay. Use a knitting needle or similar tool to burnish the back of the print onto the clay. Leave for about an hour on a tile or piece of glass.

Place the cubes in a preheated oven at 266°F/130°C, and set the timer for 5 minutes. After 5 minutes, remove one of the pieces and carefully peel back the corner of the transfer image. If the image has transferred successfully the paper will have no image on it as the picture will have been transferred to the clay. Remove the blank paper.

Return the piece to the oven to complete the full bake time. When cool, wet-sand the edges if necessary. Apply a light coat of polish to protect the transferred image.

Stamped butterfly beads strung with silver ring beads onto a twisted linen cord.

RUBBER STAMPING

RUBBER STAMPS CAN BE USED TO apply an inked image to the surface of raw or baked clay or to impress a textured image into soft clay, as with these beads. To avoid distorting the bead when the stamp is impressed, cover a baked core bead or a wooden bead with a coat of soft clay. Here, Fimo Puppen polymer clay, a doll modeling clay, has been used, as it has a smooth, porcelain appearance when baked. The rubber stamp, a butterfly, is shown on the right.

1 COVERING THE BEAD CORE

Roll out a sheet of Puppen polymer clay on the pasta machine until it is ¹⁄₁₆–¹⁄₈" (2–3 mm) thick. Cut out two circles of clay with the cookie cutter and place one on the base of the baked bead core or wooden bead and one on top of the bead. Wrap the clay around the bead and smooth the join with your fingers. Reshape the ball by rolling it in the palm of your hands. If necessary, use a little liquid clay to help the outer raw clay stick to the baked bead core.

TOOLS & MATERIALS

- Fimo Puppen polymer clay
- ¾" (18 mm) diameter baked bead cores or wooden beads
- Pasta machine
- 1¼" (30 mm) round cookie cutter
- Liquid polymer clay
- Paintbrush handle or similar
- Rubber stamp
- Ink pad
- Dust mask
- Small brush
- Iridescent powder
- Water-based acrylic floor polish

STAMPING THE CLAY

Place the bead on a paintbrush handle. Ink the rubber stamp and press the stamp onto the clay. Slightly "roll" the stamp as you press it around the bead. Repeat to make two more butterflies around the bead. If the ink smudges, use a small brush and a little water to clean up the image. Leave the ink to dry for an hour or so.

PAINTING THE BEAD

Wearing a dust mask, use a small brush to "paint" the wings of the butterflies with iridescent powder. Bake the beads (see page 17). Leave to cool, then apply a coat of polish to the bead in two stages—first over the butterflies, then over the whole bead, leaving the polish to dry between applications.

▶ **SEE ALSO** ▶ *Baking, page 17* ▶ *Cutting and slicing, page 28* ▶ *Making a bead core, page 56*

Flat, oval Mokume Gane beads, threaded onto a black rubber cord.

A selection of Mokume Gane beads: rounds, tubes, curved tubes *(right)*, and dome-shaped *(far right)*.

MOKUME GANE

PRONOUNCED "MO-KOO-MAY GAR-NAY," this is a Japanese metalworking technique, where layers of metal are sliced through to create patterns like the wood grain in timber. It is ideally suited to polymer clay.

Many polymer-clay artists have expanded on this technique, using layers of solid color or translucent clay with foils, paints, and powders to spectacular effect. The basic technique involves several thinly rolled layers of clay that are stacked on top of each other and then distorted by pressing into them with tools. When the stack is sliced through, extraordinary patterns are revealed. Added depth is achieved by using translucent clays, sometimes tinted with a pinch of colored clay or metallic mica clays.

Order of stacking
Black sheet
Silver mica sheet
Black sheet
Gold mica sheet
Copper mica sheet

TOOLS & MATERIALS
- Polymer clay—black, gold mica, silver mica, and copper mica
- Ripple blade
- Craft knife
- Roller or pasta machine
- Needle tool

▶ **Tip**
▶ To prevent the thin clay tearing, whether rolling by hand or pasta machine, sandwich the clay between two sheets of baking parchment.

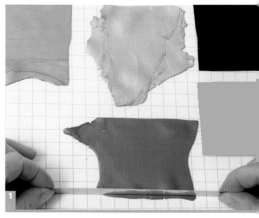

CUTTING THE SQUARES
Roll out all the clay using a roller or on a thin setting on a pasta machine. Cut two squares of black and one of each of the other clays and lay them on your work surface.

ROLLING THE STACKS
Put one half on top of the other keeping the same sequence of layers. Roll to reduce the thickness by half.

Flat Mokume Gane beads threaded with black disk beads and bought gold spacer beads.

STACKING THE SQUARES
Lay the silver clay square on one of the black squares, lowering one edge first then the rest of the square.

REMOVING AIR POCKETS
Use a craft knife to puncture air bubbles and gently roll the clay with the roller.

BUILDING UP LAYERS
Now lay the other black square on the silver and roll again. Lay the gold sheet and then copper on the stack. Roll to reduce the thickness by half. Use a blade to halve the stack.

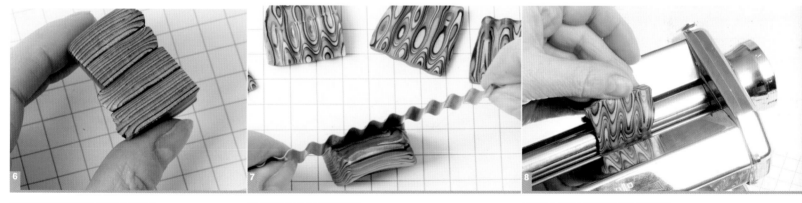

COMPRESSING THE STACK
Repeat Step 5 twice but on the last time do not reduce the thickness. Begin to compress the stack into a neat block (any distortion will help create interesting strata within).

SLICING THE STACKS
Leave the clay block to cool as it will be very soft after all the handling. Then turn the stack on its side and, using a ripple blade, slice downward making slices about ⅛" (4 mm) thick. Keep slicing off parts of the stack.

USING THE PASTA MACHINE
Roll the slices with a roller or use the medium setting on the pasta machine (depending on which way you feed the slice into the machine it will lengthen or widen the pattern). The slices are now ready to make into shaped beads.

▶ **SEE ALSO** ▷ Using a pasta machine, page 14 ▶ Making logs and sheets, page 18 ▶ Mica-shift technique, page 66

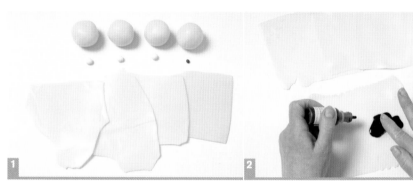

Two rounds and one lentil in translucent Mokume Gane.

The clay for these beads was patterned by cutting into the layered clay stack with a crinkle cutter tool.

Triangular-shaped beads in translucent clay strung together like arrowheads.

MOKUME GANE USING TRANSLUCENT CLAY

ONE OF THE MOST EFFECTIVE WAYS to use translucent clay is following the Mokume Gane technique. By stacking thin layers of translucent clay alternately with sheets of metallic leaf and then distressing the stack to distort the layers inside, you will reveal exciting and unexpected patterns when the stack is cut into slices. The translucent clay can either be tinted or you can use a different-colored background onto which the slices are laid. Sanding and buffing will heighten the translucency of the clay and give greater depth to the layers beneath the surface.

TOOLS & MATERIALS

- Polymer clay—Premo Frost, white, and purple
- Black acrylic paint
- Silver leaf
- Glitter
- Pearl clay
- Pasta machine
- Paintbrush
- Brayer or acrylic roller
- Impressing tool
- Tissue blade
- Baking parchment
- Triangular cookie cutter
- Piece of paper for baking
- Needle tool
- 400–800-grit wet and dry sandpapers
- Water-based acrylic floor polish
- Ranger's Poly-Glaze

1

MAKING THE MIXES

Roll four 1" (25 mm) balls of translucent clay. Mix a ³⁄₁₆" (5 mm) ball of white clay into three of the balls. Mix a peppercorn-size ball of purple clay into the fourth ball. Roll all four balls into sheets on the thinnest setting of the pasta machine. Place the three whitened sheets to one side.

2

PAINTING THE PURPLE SHEET

Using either your finger or a paintbrush, paint the purple tinted sheet with black paint. Leave to dry.

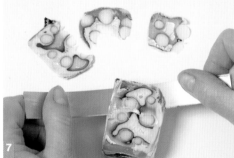

7

SLICING THE STACK

Press the stack firmly onto the work surface. Hold a tissue blade with both hands so it bends and cut very thin slices off the stack.

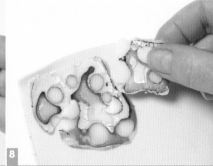

8

ROLLING THE BASE CLAY

Roll out the pearl clay to make a medium thick sheet, then lay the cut slices on top of the pearl clay, overlapping them slightly. Place a piece of baking parchment over the slices and roll with a roller or brayer to flatten the slices into the pearl clay.

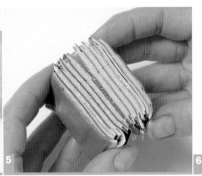

ADDING FOIL AND GLITTER

Lay a sheet of silver leaf onto two of the white tinted sheets and smooth down. Tear off eight ½" (12 mm) squares from the third white sheet and roll them into balls for use later. Pour some glitter over the remainder of the third sheet and use a roller to press the glitter into the surface.

STACKING THE SHEETS

Tear or cut all the full sheets of clay into 2½" (63 mm) squares and lay them out individually. Build a stack by alternating silver, glitter, silver, and black sheets. Continue stacking, keeping the sequence until the last piece, which should be placed with its translucent face on top.

HALVING THE STACK

Divide the stack in half and place the bottom half on top of the top half.

IMPRESSING THE STACK

Use an impressing tool or the end of a paintbrush to make indentations of different depths into the stack. Take care not to press right through the stack. Fill the holes with the small balls you made earlier. Turn the stack over, make more holes, and fill them as before.

Compress the stack with your hands to distort the interior, make interesting strata, and stick all the layers together.

> ▶ **Tip**
> ▶ The beads need to be sealed to prevent the silver leaf from tarnishing later. Here, a coat of glaze has been applied to each side. Any valleys in the surface of the clay will be filled and the beads will be given an illusion of depth. When dry, seal with acrylic polish.

A variety of beads made with translucent clays and foils.

CUTTING OUT SHAPES

Using a cookie cutter, cut out shapes from the most interesting part of the decorative sheet. Place two pieces back to back.

BAKING AND FINISHING

Make the thread hole with a needle tool and bake the pieces lying flat on a piece of paper (see page 17). After baking, wet-sand the edges and finish as you wish.

▶ **SEE ALSO** ▶ Baking, page 17 ▶ Varnishing, page 49 ▶ Texturing, page 55 ▶ Mokume Gane, page 62

A necklace of square beads with a holographic-effect pattern, threaded with thin, curved, metal beads.

A necklace of pointed, silver beads. Notice that the curved beads are threaded alternately.

MICA SHIFT EFFECT

METALLIC POLYMER CLAYS ARE FILLED with tiny mica particles. These particles can be aligned in one direction by rolling several times through a pasta machine, placing the clay in the same direction with each pass. When light reflects off the aligned mica, the material seems to have a metallic quality. More surprising effects are produced by distorting the aligned particles, which disturbs the reflective mica bits within the clay. This can be done by impressing a texture sheet, a rubber stamp, or a ball stylus into the clay. Even when the surface is sliced away the image of the impressed texture remains. The new surface is flat, yet an apparently three-dimensional pattern is still visible. This holographic effect is known as mica shift.

Gold, silver, copper, and pearl are available as mica clays. Mixing any plain colored clay with one of these mica clays will immediately enliven the appearance of the plain clay. Try this with scrap clay, and the mica particles will turn a "mud" colored clay into something quite unexpected and interesting, often creating a very usable clay. Sanding and buffing will always enhance the mica shift effect to its full potential.

TOOLS & MATERIALS

- Polymer clay—gold or another mica clay
- Roller or pasta machine
- Texture sheet, rubber stamp, or impressing tool
- Water spray (release agent)
- Tissue blade
- Acrylic roller or brayer
- Needle tool
- 400–800-grit wet and dry sandpapers
- 1" (25 mm) square cookie cutter for beads
- Buffing machine or cotton or denim polishing cloth

ROLLING THE CLAY
To align the mica particles, roll the clay through a pasta machine on the thickest setting, folding the clay and rolling through in the same direction each time. Do this several times.

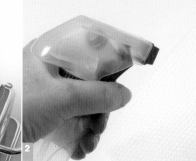

PREPARING THE SHEET
Spray a flexible plastic texture sheet with water to keep it from sticking to the clay. You can use either side. Alternatively, you can use a rubber stamp or impressing tool.

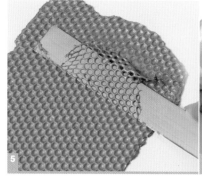

SLICING THE CLAY
Hold the tissue blade parallel to the clay surface and slice off the textured clay in one long, even slice, if possible. Save the shavings as these can be used as decoration on a bead or flipped over and rolled onto another sheet of gold mica clay.

JOINING THE SHEETS
Using a roller or pasta machine, roll a thick sheet of gold clay. Lay the shaved imprinted sheet on top of the gold clay, image side up.

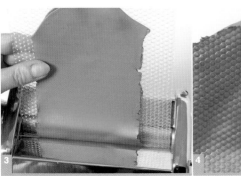

IMPRESSING THE CLAY

Lay the clay onto a wetted texture sheet and roll lengthwise through the pasta machine on the thickest setting. Carefully separate the clay from the texture sheet and lay the clay, textured side up, on a firm flat surface.

THE IMPRESSIONS

Impressions taken from both sides of the plastic texture sheet.

EXPELLING THE AIR

Use a roller or brayer to flatten any raised areas and to expel trapped air. You can use the pasta machine but this may stretch the image.

CUTTING OUT SHAPES

Cut out the bead shapes with a cookie cutter. Place two squares back to back so the mica-shift image is visible on both sides. Make a thread hole, bake, and finish as desired.

MICA SHIFT RIPPLE BLADE EFFECT

TOOLS & MATERIALS
- Polymer clay—silver mica
- Roller or pasta machine
- Fine ripple blade
- Tissue blade
- Needle tool
- Paper concertina bead holder

CREATING A STACK

Roll out sheets on a pasta machine, to condition the clay and align the mica particles. Place sheets together to make a stack about 2" (50 mm) square and ¾" (18 mm) thick. Keep the sheets aligned, and smooth out any air pockets.

Place the stack on its side on the work surface. Cut a ⅛" (3 mm) slice downward with the ripple blade.

MAKING THREAD HOLES

Slightly curve each triangle and pierce two of the corners with the needle tool to make the thread holes. To maintain the curve in the triangles while baking, lay the pieces in a folded paper cradle, then bake (see page 17).

ROLLING AND CUTTING

Roll the slices through the pasta machine on the thickest setting, keeping the ripple blade lines perpendicular to the rollers. Reduce the setting by one and roll again, keeping the lines perpendicular to the rollers. Continue to reduce the setting and roll the clay through until it is of a medium thickness.

Using the straight tissue blade, cut triangles out of the clay.

▶ **SEE ALSO** ▶ *Using a pasta machine, page 14* ▶ *Cutting and slicing, page 28*

FAUX

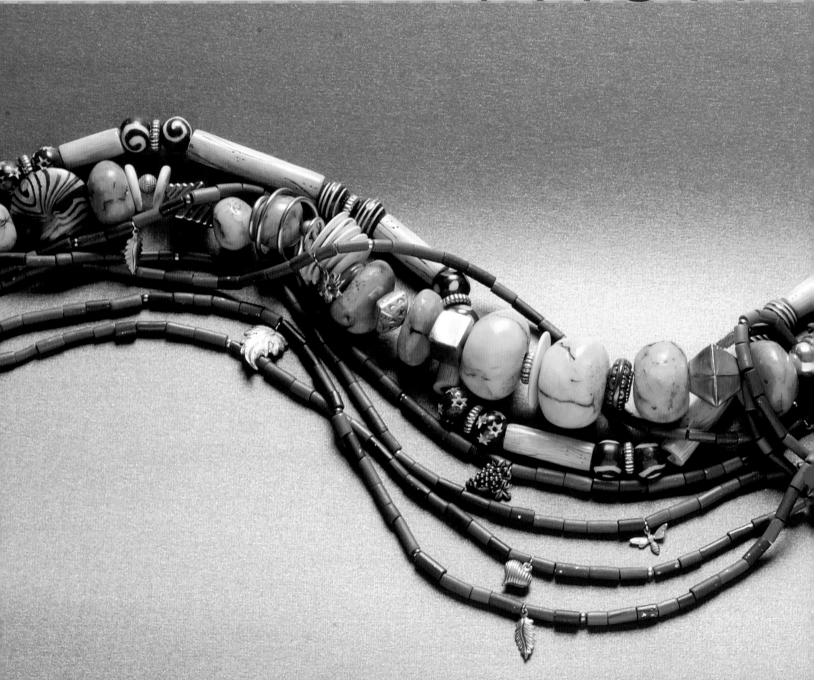

TECHNIQUES

A few pieces of gold leaf were mixed into the clay to add sparkle in these flat, oval beads.

A pair of earrings, each made from two domed pieces of faux wood clay, joined together to form lentil beads.

WOOD

THERE ARE MANY DIFFERENT TYPES of wood effects that you can make out of polymer clay. Experiment with the colors or the thickness of the sheets of clay to change the end result. For this exotic "zebrawood," the key ingredients are contrasting colors of clay to emphasize the grain pattern of the wood. Whatever the wood type, at least one of the polymer clays should include a mica clay to give the distinctive sheen of wood that has been sliced across the grain.

TOOLS & MATERIALS

- Polymer clay—gold mica and dark brown
- Dark brown scrap clay
- Liquid polymer clay
- Roller or pasta machine
- Tissue blade
- Brayer or roller
- 1½" (38 mm) round cookie cutter
- Escargot serving tray (an old light bulb or the back of a soup spoon may be substituted)
- Craft knife
- Needle tool
- 400–800-grit wet and dry sandpaper
- Piece of denim for satin finish

ROLLING THE CLAY SHEETS

Roll the gold clay several times using a roller or on the thickest setting of a pasta machine to align the mica particles. Also roll the dark brown clay. Using a tissue blade, cut the gold clay into a strip. Place on top of the dark brown sheet and trim the edges so both colors are equal in size.

REMOVING AIR POCKETS

Use a roller to expel any air, then roll the clay lengthwise using a roller or on the thickest pasta machine setting.

ADDING THE BACKING

To make your "wood veneer" go farther, roll out a backing sheet of dark brown scrap clay to a medium thickness. Lay the "wood" slices next to each other on top of the backing sheet. Roll this through the thickest setting on the pasta machine.

CUTTING OUT THE BEADS

Reduce the setting on the pasta machine and roll again. Repeat, rolling the clay sheet to reach the desired thickness—here it has been rolled four times. Find an interesting section on the sheet, and using a cutter, cut out circles for the beads.

A necklace of small cube beads with veneers of faux wood, strung with gold metal beads.

MAKING A JELLY ROLL

With the gold side facing upward, use the tissue blade to cut the short edges at an angle to expose the brown clay. Roll the clay with the gold on the inside to make a jelly roll. Ensure no gold shows at the end join; press to seal the seam.

MAKING THE SQUARE CANE

Use a roller to slightly flatten the jelly roll along the full length of the cane. Turn the clay onto its side and roll the second side. Continue turning the clay and rolling until it is in the shape of a short square cane. Leave the cane to cool.

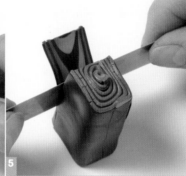

SLICING THE CANE

Stand the cane on one end and use a tissue blade to cut a downward slice ⅛" (3 mm) thick to reveal the "wood grain" inside. Cut several more slices.

ROLLING THE SLICES

Roll each slice lengthwise using a roller or the thickest setting on the pasta machine. Turn down the setting by one and roll the slices through again. Repeat. To widen the slice, turn it by 90° before rolling through.

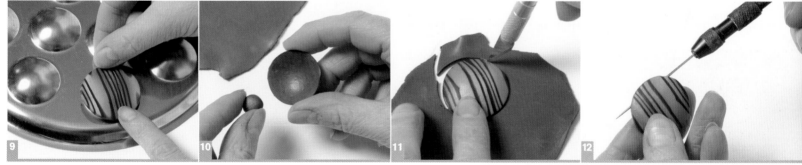

CURVING THE BEAD

To give the bead a domed shape, place the cut-out circle on the back of an escargot serving tray. Bake (see page 17). When cool, remove from the tray and coat the edge and inside of the pieces with liquid polymer clay.

KEEPING THE DOMED SHAPE

Place a ball of scrap clay inside the baked domed clay to prevent it from sagging during the next baking. The finished bead will have a domed front and a flat back.

MAKING THE BACKING

Place the bead on a medium thick sheet of dark brown scrap clay and cut around it with a craft knife. Alternatively, put two domes together around a ball of scrap clay to make a double-sided lentil bead.

FINISHING THE BEAD

Make a thread hole with a needle tool and rebake. Alternatively, rebake and then make a thread hole with a hand drill. Wet-sand the beads with 400–800-grit sandpaper. Buff with a piece of denim for a satin finish.

▶ **SEE ALSO** ▶ Using a pasta machine, page 14 ▶ Baking, page 17 ▶ Cutting and slicing, page 28 ▶ Caning and stacking, page 30

VEINED MARBLE

MARBLE FORMS IN A GEOLOGICAL process that needs heat and pressure and takes millions of years to create. This polymer clay project takes just a couple of hours.

There are thousands of types of marble and hard stones used for beads. Real stone bead shapes are usually very simple balls, cubes, and cylinders that suit a hard and brittle material like marble. The tetrahedron shape used here is rather unusual, but it's definitely suited to marble. Add plenty of translucent clay to any marble mix as this gives depth to each "stone." Adding pearl powder creates the "gritty" appearance that marble sometimes has.

TOOLS & MATERIALS

- Polymer clay—white and translucent
- Sparkling pearl powder with built-in resin
- Polymer clay softener
- Raw umber acrylic paint
- Black acrylic paint
- Tissue blade or craft knife
- Piece of paper
- Smooth wooden block
- Needle tool
- Stiff paintbrush
- Tile or piece of card stock
- 240–800-grit wet and dry sandpapers
- Buffing machine or denim buffing cloth (optional)

CUTTING THE CLAY

Chop equal amounts of white and translucent clay into chunks using a tissue blade or craft knife.

ADDING SPARKLE

Sprinkle some sparkling pearl powder over the chopped clay.

SHAPING THE CLAY

Make a tetrahedron—a four-sided shape—from one of the portions of clay by pinching into shape with your thumbs and index fingers. Repeat for the other beads.

MAKING THE EDGES STRAIGHT

Use a smooth wooden block to flatten and straighten the sides and edges of each bead.

A necklace *(left)* and earrings *(far right)* of veined marble with varnished black polymer clay spacer beads.

REMOISTENING THE CLAY

As the powder tends to dry out the clay, add a few drops of clay softener to remoisten the clay. Mix and press together and then chop into large and small pieces.

COLORING THE CLAY

Mix together raw umber and black acrylic paint and apply with a paintbrush to thoroughly cover all the clay pieces.

LETTING THE PAINT DRY

Leave the painted pieces to dry on a clean piece of paper for about 20 minutes. Then divide them into several bead-size portions.

A variety of veined faux marble beads in different colors and shapes.

MAKING THE THREAD HOLE

With a needle tool, make the hole for the thread. Here the bead has been pierced from the center of one edge, across the bead, exiting at the center of the opposite edge. Bake the beads on a tile or a piece of card stock (see page 17).

SANDING AND BUFFING

When the beads have cooled, wet-sand with a range of 240–800-grit sandpapers. Then, if you have a buffing machine, buff the beads to emphasize the translucency and sparkle, or handpolish with denim for a satin finish.

▶ **SEE ALSO** ▶ *Baking, page 17* ▶ *Sanding and polishing, page 48*

A necklace of flat, irregular faux ivory pieces showing signs of "age" and "wear."

A multistranded necklace of different-size tube beads, patterned, patinated, and threaded with gold metal beads *(right)*.

IVORY AND BONE

BOTH BONE AND IVORY have long been used for jewelry charms and beads. Although different materials, they share a characteristic straight grain—similar to wood—and a beautiful translucency enhanced by natural oils from frequent handling and wearing next to the skin.

Hollow bones are often carved or pierced to reveal their interiors whereas ivory beads tend to be solid with a more visible grain structure. Both materials develop fine cracks along the grain, which become more visible with age and use.

TOOLS & MATERIALS
- Polymer clay—ecru or beige, white, and translucent
- Dark brown acrylic paint
- Roller or pasta machine
- Tissue blade
- Paper to build bead on
- Bamboo skewer or wooden dowel
- Needle tool
- Paper adhesive glue
- Ball stylus or thin knitting needle
- 800-grit wet and dry sandpaper
- Stiff paintbrush
- Paper towel
- Cotton cloth for buffing

An ethnic-style necklace of tube beads in different lengths threaded with small, carved beads.

ROLLING THE CLAY SHEETS

Mix equal parts of ecru and white clay together and roll into a sheet using a roller or on a medium setting on a pasta machine. Roll out two parts of the translucent clay on the same setting.

Carefully lay one sheet on top of the other—if you start from one end you should avoid air bubbles. Roll the stacked clay using the roller or on the thickest setting of the pasta machine. Using a tissue blade, trim to make a rectangular shape.

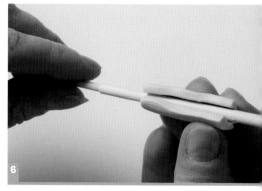

FORMING THE TUBE

Press the clay slice around the paper sleeve and neatly butt the edges together. Roll the tube across a clean work surface to smooth the join.

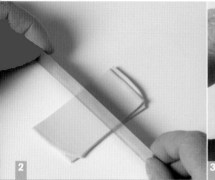

2

BUILDING UP LAYERS

With a tissue blade, cut the sheet in half and stack one sheet on top of the other, so the clay is four layers thick and the layers are alternating in color. Halve and stack two more times, being careful to expel any air pockets.

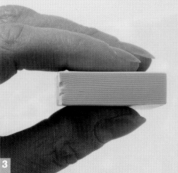

3

THE STACK

You should have a total of 16 layers. Continue to halve and stack if necessary to suit your project.

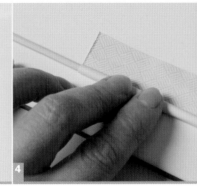

4

MAKING A SLEEVE

To make a bone tube bead, first create a paper sleeve. Wrap a rectangular sheet of paper around a bamboo skewer or wooden dowel and glue in place. The paper sleeve should be wider than the bead, to ease later handling.

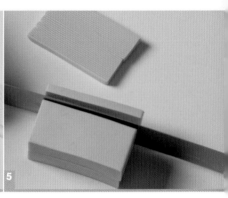

5

CUTTING A SLICE

Using a tissue blade, cut a ⅛" (3 mm) thick slice through the layers of the stack.

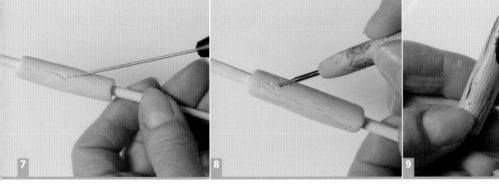

7

AUTHENTICATING THE EFFECT

With a needle tool, draw on lines to mimic cracks and scratches.

8

SIMULATING PORES

Make marks with a ball stylus or point of a small knitting needle to simulate the pores found in real bone. Bake the beads (see page 17), then soak in water to remove the paper sleeve.

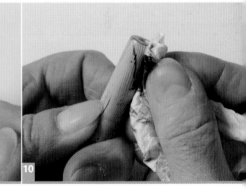

9

COLORING THE BEAD

Wet-sand with 800-grit sandpaper. Then, using a paintbrush, paint the bead with dark brown acrylic paint to give an antique look.

10

COMPLETING THE EFFECT

Immediately wipe off most of the paint with a paper towel, leaving it only in the crevices. Finish the bead by buffing with a cotton cloth to give a soft sheen.

▶ **SEE ALSO** ▶ Using a pasta machine, page 14 ▶ Baking, page 17 ▶ Cutting and slicing, page 28 ▶ Caning and stacking, page 30

A necklace of many richly textured faux leather pieces, some with imitation stitching.

A faux leather strap *(right)*.

Rolled faux leather beads and coco chips threaded on a knotted leather cord *(far right)*.

LEATHER

POLYMER CLAY LENDS ITSELF well to replicating the look, texture, and color of leather. The texture of leather can be reproduced in several ways. Pressing scrunched-up aluminum foil into the clay gives an interesting random effect that is enhanced by patinating with a wash of acrylic paint. Or you could try pressing a real piece of coarse-grained leather into the clay. As always with natural materials, the faux effect is more convincing if you can vary the color of some of the beads.

TOOLS & MATERIALS
- Polymer clay—several browns
- Burnt umber acrylic paint
- Black acrylic paint
- Roller or pasta machine
- Piece of aluminum foil
- Triangular template
- Tissue blade
- Bamboo skewer or wooden dowel
- Stiff paintbrush
- Paper towel
- Water-based acrylic floor polish (optional)

Faux leather tassels

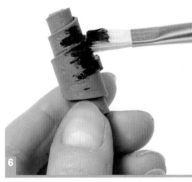

1

ROLLING THE CLAY
Roll several different brown clay sheets using a roller or on a medium setting on a pasta machine.

2

CREATING TEXTURE
Scrunch up a piece of aluminum foil and press into the clay sheets to create a texture on the entire sheet.

6

PAINTING THE BEAD
When the baked bead is cool, apply a mix of burnt umber and black acrylic paint with a paintbrush.

7

ENHANCING THE TEXTURE
Wipe the paint off immediately with a paper towel, leaving some in the crevices to define the edges and accentuate the texture. Apply a light coat of water-based acrylic floor polish to give the bead a slight sheen.

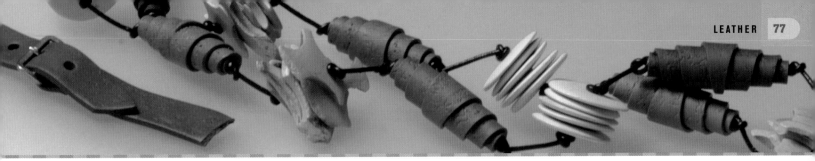

CUTTING OUT THE CLAY SHAPE

Place the template on an interestingly textured part of the clay and cut out the shape using a tissue blade.

ROLLING UP THE CLAY

Carefully turn the clay over and, starting at the broader end of the clay, roll the clay onto a bamboo skewer or wooden dowel.

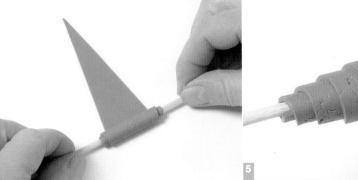

THE ROLLED BEAD

Continue rolling the clay until all the clay is rolled around the skewer or dowel, then bake (see page 17).

MAKING A FAUX LEATHER TASSEL

MAKING THE TASSEL

Roll a medium-thick sheet of brown clay and texture it using aluminum foil. Turn the sheet over and cut out a rectangle 1¼" x 3" (30 x 75 mm). Using a tissue blade, cut the tassel "skirt." Place a piece of wire at one end of the clay and roll to form a tassel. Do not remove the wire.

FINISHING THE TASSEL

Using a needle tool, make marks in the clay to imitate stitching. Bake the tassel resting on polyester fiberfill. After the beads have cooled, use a mix of black and burnt umber acrylic paint to accentuate the "leather" texture.

A richly decorated talisman necklace of amulets and charms, tassels, and faux leather pouches, as well as pieces of faux coral, ivory, amber, and agate.

▶ **SEE ALSO** ▶ Using a pasta machine, page 14 ▶ Making logs and sheets, page 18 ▶ Varnishing, page 49

AMBER

REAL AMBER IS A FOSSIL RESIN that oozed from ancient pinelike trees up to sixty million years ago. Sometimes it is found as a clear, honeylike deposit with seeds and insects trapped in the resin; but when used as beads it is more often a cloudy yellow-orange, ranging in tone from pale cream to dark burnt orange.

In this cloudy, translucent form the beads are round and chunky. As a relatively soft material, amber beads do show signs of wear and usage, but their cracks and scratches add a pleasing character. Today, many amber beads are, in fact, plastic imitations, so you are following a long tradition in making your own imitations. Try to vary the individual bead colors to add realism.

TOOLS & MATERIALS

- Polymer clay—translucent, sunflower-yellow, wine-red, and lemon-yellow
- Scrap clay (optional)
- Burnt umber acrylic paint
- Tissue blade
- Grater
- Craft knife
- Coarse sandpaper for texturing
- Needle tool
- 800-grit wet and dry sandpaper
- Stiff paintbrush
- Paper towel
- Cotton or denim buffing cloth

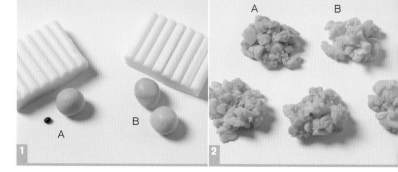

MAKING THE MIXES

Make a dark amber polymer clay mixture (A) using ten parts translucent to one part sunflower-yellow and a speck of wine-red. Make a paler amber clay mixture (B) using ten parts translucent to one part each of sunflower and lemon yellow.

APPORTIONING THE CLAY

Chop up the A and B mixes with a tissue blade, keeping them in separate heaps. Set aside two bead-size quantities of A and of B to use for the darkest and lightest beads. Mix up the remainder of the heaps to make up the different tones of beads in between.

TEXTURING AND BAKING

Use very coarse sandpaper sparingly, to texture the clay to simulate wear and age for a natural appearance. Pierce the bead with a needle tool to make the threading hole, then bake the bead (see page 17). When the bead is cool, wet-sand with 800-grit sandpaper, using plenty of water.

A decorative necklace of faux amber pieces threaded with other polymer clay beads, including a wound faux wire bead made from extruded gold clay.

GRATING THE CLAY

Press a chopped heap portion together and grate coarsely.

FORMING THE BEAD

Take a ball of light-colored scrap clay and press the gratings around it, letting some cracks and creases remain between the gratings. (Scrap clay is optional, but it does make the amber mix go farther.)

AUTHENTICATING THE EFFECT

Use a craft knife to emphasize a few cracks by twisting the knife into the bead a couple of times to get an uneven appearance.

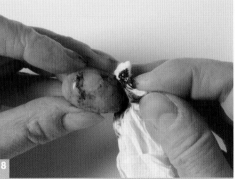

PAINTING THE BEAD

Use a paintbrush to paint undiluted burnt umber acrylic paint into the crevices.

COMPLETING THE LOOK

Immediately wipe the paint off with a paper towel, leaving paint in the crevices. Buff with a cotton cloth or a piece of denim to enhance the translucency of the bead.

Varying the proportions of the colors mixed, and the different sizes and shapes made, as in natural amber, will result in beads with more realism.

▶ **SEE ALSO** ▶ *Baking, page 17* ▶ *Mixing color, page 20* ▶ *Sanding and polishing, page 48*

A necklace of random lengths of faux branch coral threaded with small silver ring beads.

CORAL

CORAL IS THE OUTER SKELETONS of colonies of sea creatures. It is often capable of retaining a bright color and of taking a high polish. Branch coral is just one of many species of endangered coral, and its bright red and orange colors have made it highly prized for jewelry. Do not contribute to the destruction of coral reefs—make your own coral instead.

For this type of coral, a clay extruder tool has been used. This lends the coral a consistent and credible character, but you can also roll your own lengths of clay to form branch coral. Fimo Soft clay is used here as it is easier to extrude.

▶ **Tip**
▶ Most polymer clay reds, such as raspberry, will quickly overpower other colors in a mix so use sparingly.

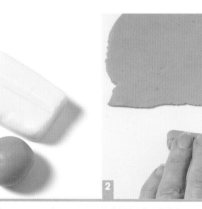

1

MAKING THE MIX
Mix four parts translucent clay with two parts each of tangerine and sunflower-yellow and one part each of raspberry and white. Mix small batches, slightly varying the amounts in each batch.

2

ROLLING LOGS
Leave the final mixes a little streaky to imitate natural variations. Roll the batches of clay into logs the right size for the extruder tool.

6

TEXTURING
Texture the raw clay with coarse sandpaper on a few exposed areas and add some cracks and scratches with a craft knife.

7

MAKING THE THREAD HOLE
With a needle tool, make a thread hole through the center top or along the length of the coral bead, then bake (see page 17). Leave to cool, then sand with 800-grit sandpaper.

TOOLS & MATERIALS
- Polymer clay—tangerine, sunflower-yellow, raspberry, translucent, and white
- Brown acrylic paint
- Clay extruder tool with ¼" (6 mm) circular die hole
- Coarse sandpaper for texturing
- Craft knife
- Needle tool
- 800-grit wet and dry sandpaper
- Stiff paintbrush
- Paper towel
- Water-based acrylic floor polish

A necklace threaded with beads of
different materials, including seashells, which
complement the pieces of faux coral.

LOADING THE EXTRUDER TOOL
Put one of the logs into the barrel
of the extruder tool.

EXTRUDING LENGTHS OF CLAY
Extrude 1½–2" (38–50 mm) lengths of clay
and carefully break them off. Note that the
extrusion flows more easily if the clay and
the extruder tool are slightly warm.

MAKING THE CORAL
Hand mold and pinch the
lengths of clay to create
buds and stubby branches
of coral.

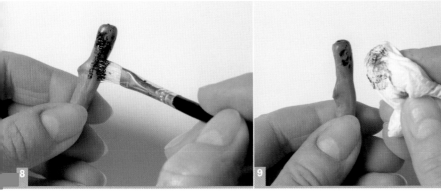

STIPPLING
With a paintbrush, stipple dark brown
acrylic paint over the textured areas.

FINISHING TOUCHES
Wipe the paint off immediately with a paper
towel, leaving paint in the cracks and scratches.
Use water-based acrylic floor polish to give
a pleasing sheen.

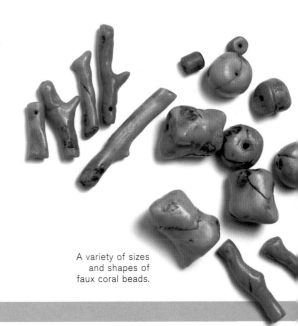

A variety of sizes
and shapes of
faux coral beads.

▶ **SEE ALSO** ▶ *Baking, page 17* ▶ *Mixing color, page 20* ▶ *Varnishing, page 49*

A necklace threaded with many different bead shapes all imitating bronze but made from scrap clay decorated with metallic powder.

BRONZE

BRONZE HAS BEEN USED TO MAKE BEADS since people have worked with metal—in fact, since the Bronze Age. Both bronze and brass are copper-rich alloys. Smaller quantities of zinc (in brass) or tin (in bronze) vary the color and working properties of the alloys. Polished bronze has a golden color, which tarnishes through brown to dark red and eventually green. The distinctive pale green patina that develops on old bronze is called verdigris.

Faux "bronze" is a good opportunity to use up scrap clay. Metallic powders applied to the high points of a dark clay mix will suggest bright polished parts on an old metal bead, but you can also use ready-mixed metallic polymer clays made with mica. Polymer clay replicas are more convincing when they echo the cast shapes of real metal beads, often from Africa and Asia, or you could invent a shape that suits metal, such as the "lantern" bead shown here.

TOOLS & MATERIALS

- A mix of dark scrap clay
- Gold mica polymer clay
- Bronze pearl powder
- Acrylic paint—turquoise, yellow ocher, black, and white
- Roller or pasta machine
- Paper to build beads on
- ¼" (6 mm) diameter metal rod or wooden dowel
- Paper adhesive
- Craft knife
- Tissue blade
- Soft brush
- Dust mask
- Water-based acrylic floor polish
- Paintbrush
- Paper towel

Patinated beads.

ROLLING THE CLAY
Collect some predominantly dark scrap clay and roll with a roller or brayer until it can be rolled through on the thickest setting of a pasta machine.

ADDING SPARKLE
Mix the scrap clay sheet with some gold mica clay for a metallic sparkle. Add darker clay if the mix seems too light. Roll with a roller or on a medium setting of a pasta machine until it is about ⅟₁₆" (2 mm) thick.

CUTTING THE BEAD
With a craft knife, make evenly spaced 1" (25 mm) parallel cuts along the center part of the tube.

STRETCHING THE BEAD
Grasp the paper sleeves and gently pull them slightly apart so you stretch the clay at the center of the tube.

MAKING THE PAPER SLEEVES

Wrap and glue two paper sleeves onto a rod or dowel, about ¼" (6 mm) in diameter. Push the paper sleeves together into the center of the dowel.

WRAPPING UP THE CLAY

Cut a strip 2½" (63 mm) wide. Trim the leading edge of the clay with a tissue blade and place the rod or dowel onto it.

FORMING THE BEAD

Wrap the clay one turn around the rod or dowel and, with a tissue blade, cut the clay so that the edges meet.

ROLLING OUT THE BEAD

Press the cut edges of the clay together and roll back and forth on a smooth work surface to blend the seam of the tube.

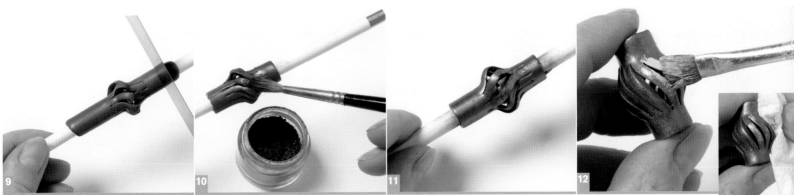

THE BALLOON EFFECT

When the paper sleeves are pushed back together the stretched and cut clay will balloon outward. Give the tubes a twist to add interest to the balloon shape. Trim the ends with a tissue blade so that they are pleasantly proportioned.

APPLYING BRONZE COLOR

Put on a dust mask. Using a soft, dry brush, dust the unbaked clay with bronze pearl powdered pigment, working over a piece of paper to catch the loose powder. Brush off the excess powder.

BAKING AND VARNISHING

Bake the bead on the rod (see page 17). When cool, soak the bead in water to remove the paper sleeves. Seal the metallic powder with a thin coat of water-based acrylic floor polish to stop any powder from rubbing off.

PAINTING ON VERDIGRIS

Mix the acrylic paint to make a pale green/blue to simulate verdigris and brush into the recesses of the bead with a paintbrush. Almost immediately wipe off most of the paint with a paper towel before it dries.

▶ **SEE ALSO** ▶ Using a pasta machine, page 14 ▶ Baking, page 17 ▶ Cutting and slicing, page 28 ▶ Varnishing, page 49

Large pieces of faux abalone shell
threaded on a silver chain.

ABALONE

THIS "FAUX" ABALONE TECHNIQUE exploits
the shimmering characteristics of pearl
clay. Up to six colors are used for this
multilayered effect, while interlayers of black
painted clay and abalone foil give additional
definition. It uses a brighter palette than
mother-of-pearl (see page 88).

The foil is not essential, but when
it is revealed by the slicing it will
glisten beautifully.

TOOLS & MATERIALS

- Polymer clay—pearl, purple, cobalt blue,
  turquoise, sea-green, zinc-yellow with a
  hint of cobalt blue, fuchsia
- Liquid polymer clay
- Black oil paint
- Roller or pasta machine
- Tile or piece of glass for mixing
  paint on
- Cherry or orange stick
- Stiff paintbrush
- Crafter's metal foil—
  abalone or gold (optional)
- Food processor (optional)
- Tissue blade
- Ball stylus
- Polyester fiberfill
- Water-based acrylic
  floor polish

▶ Tip

▶ For a very shiny piece of abalone, bake
the slices face down on a tile or piece of
glass. The pieces can still be curved by
taking them out of the hot oven and then
holding them in cold water until they hold
the desired shape.

MAKING THE MIXES

Mix a 1" (25 mm) ball of pearl clay with a
¼" (6 mm) ball of colored clay. Repeat for each
type of colored clay so you have six different
colored balls. Roll each ball into a sheet.

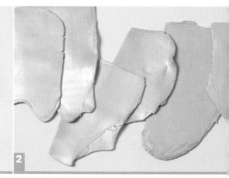

ROLLING THE CLAY

Take about a fifth of each colored sheet and
roll out very thinly using a roller or a pasta
machine. On a tile or piece of glass use a
cherry stick to mix equal amounts of liquid
polymer clay and black oil paint.

STACKING THE SHEETS

Tear the foil-backed sheets into small same-size
sheets and stack, starting with a foil-backed
sheet with the foil facing upward. Put on three
colored sheets—alternating the colors—followed
by another foil-backed sheet, then three more
colored sheets.

HALVING THE STACK

Continue stacking until all the clay sheets
have been used. Cut the stack in half using
a tissue blade; put one stack on top of the
other. Carefully compress the stack to expel
any air pockets between the layers.

A necklace of strips of faux abalone joined end to end with metal findings and two individual beads *(right)*.

PAINTING THE SHEETS

Paint each of the six very thin sheets with the liquid clay/black oil paint using a paintbrush or by smearing it with your finger. Lay each of the painted sheets paint-side down onto a sheet of metal foil. Put these aside.

CHOPPING UP THE CLAY

Chop up the unpainted colored sheets. (If possible, tear them into pieces and process for a few seconds in a food processor. This chops the clay into rounded nugget shapes without overmixing the colors.)

MAKING "PANCAKES"

Pinch the clay into "pancakes" the thickness of the thickest setting on the pasta machine and roll the clay through. Reduce the setting and roll again.

TEARING THE CLAY

Continue turning down the setting on the pasta machine and working until the clay is rolled through on the thinnest setting. Tear into small same-size sheets. (This avoids straight lines appearing in the finished beads.)

INDENTING THE CLAY

Use a ball stylus to make indents in the clay. Turn the stack over and make more indents on the other side.

COMPRESSING THE STACK

With fingers and thumbs, compress the stack again from all sides to close up all the holes and to disturb the layered strata inside. Leave the stack to rest for an hour in a cool place—this makes it easier to slice.

CUTTING SLICES

Press the stack down so that it sticks to the work surface and cannot slide around. Grasp the tissue blade with both hands. Bend the blade and slice across the top of the stack, cutting very thin slices.

BAKING AND VARNISHING

For a natural look, curve the slices and bake on polyester fiberfill (see page 17). Once baked, cut or tear to shape while still warm. Apply one coat of water-based acrylic floor polish to stop the foil from tarnishing.

▶ **SEE ALSO** ▶ *Using a pasta machine, page 14* ▶ *Baking, page 17* ▶ *Mixing color, page 20* ▶ *Caning and stacking, page 28* ▶ *Varnishing, page 49*

A large faux jade pendant formed over a wooden mold, threaded with strands of rubber cord.

A necklace of cylinder-shaped beads, decorated with a script, inspired by ancient prayer beads.

JADE

IN ITS MOST VALUED FORM, JADE is a translucent green mineral traditionally used in the Far East for objects and jewelry of the highest quality. Beads tend to be simple in shape but sometimes have carved inscriptions. Jade is extremely hard to carve, but consequently takes a high polish and is very durable. It is often mottled with subtle variations in color from pale to dark green.

Polymer clay jade is mostly translucent clay tinted with different proportions of a green base mix. When translucent fimo clay is baked, it has a tendency to plaque, showing as small moon-shaped disks inside the baked clay. This can be an advantage when imitating crystalline jade.

Dark mix

Light mix

1

MAKING THE MIXES

For the darker jade clay mix, use ¼" (6 mm) ball of chocolate with two ¼" (6 mm) balls of green and one 1" (25 mm) ball of translucent.

For the light jade clay mix, combine one ¼" (6 mm) ball of chocolate with two ¼" (6 mm) balls of green and three 1" (25 mm) balls of translucent.

TOOLS & MATERIALS
- Polymer clay—chocolate, green, translucent, black
- Dark brown acrylic paint
- Grater
- Ripple blade (optional)
- Roller or pasta machine
- Paper to build beads on
- ¼" (6 mm) diameter metal rod, wooden dowel, or bamboo skewer
- Paper adhesive
- Rubber stamp with oriental text characters
- Water spray
- Tissue blade or craft knife
- 800-grit wet and dry sandpaper
- Stiff paintbrush
- Paper towel
- Cotton or denim cloth or an electric buffing wheel

A rubber stamp with oriental script.

Teardrop-shaped beads made in faux jade clay.

5

ROLLING THE BEAD

Wrap the mottled jade mix around the paper sleeve and roll on a clean work surface to make it smooth.

6

APPLYING GRATED CLAY

Finely grate or chop a few crumbs of raw black polymer clay and press one or two bits into each bead. These represent the natural impurities found in jade.

Faux jade beads fitted with eye pins and threaded onto gold wire. Note the graining and the small black inclusions.

▶ Tip
▶ Using a ripple blade to chop clay into rounded chunks provides a natural look. A food processor will give the same effect.

MIXING THE CLAYS
Using a grater, coarsely grate both jade mixes together or chop with a ripple blade. Use three parts of the light green mix to one part of the dark green mix.

MAKING A "PANCAKE"
Pinch the grated crumbs together to make a flat "pancake" and roll flat using a roller or a pasta machine. Chop the clay again for a more mottled look if desired.

MAKING A PAPER SLEEVE
Make a paper sleeve and wrap around a metal rod, wooden dowel, or bamboo skewer. Glue in place.

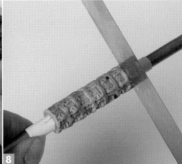

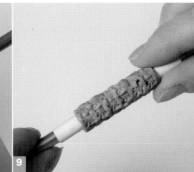

STAMPING AN IMPRESSION
Lightly spray the rubber stamp with water to prevent the clay from sticking to it. Roll the clay cylinder across the stamp, taking care not to overlap the impressions.

TIDYING THE EDGES
Trim the ends of the cylinder with a tissue blade or craft knife.

SHAPING AND SANDING
Gently pinch the ends of the bead to remove the sharpness of the edge. After baking, soak the bead in water to remove the paper sleeve. Wet-sand with 800-grit sandpaper to give the bead a harder, more carved look.

PAINTING THE BEAD
Using a stiff paintbrush, stipple dark brown paint into the indentations. Wipe off the paint with a paper towel before it dries. Buff the beads with a cloth or an electric buffing wheel to emphasize their translucency.

▶ **SEE ALSO** ▶ Baking, page 17 ▶ Mixing color, page 20

A string of faux pearls and matching earrings, graded in size, made with a white base clay ball and coated with a pearl powder finish.

Two beads inlaid with flowers of faux mother-of-pearl clay *(right)*.

A silver bracelet with leaf charms of faux mother-of-pearl *(far right)*.

MOTHER-OF-PEARL

MOTHER-OF-PEARL IS DERIVED FROM the shiny interiors of the shells of several different kinds of mollusc as well as the better-known true pearls found in oysters. This faux technique builds on the proprietary "pearl" clay made by polymer clay manufacturers, but goes further to create a really convincing effect by adding subtle tints of color. See also Abalone, page 84.

TOOLS & MATERIALS

- Polymer clay—pearl, purple, cobalt-blue, and green
- Brown acrylic paint
- Roller or pasta machine
- Tissue blade
- Brayer or acrylic roller
- Oval-or leaf-shaped cookie cutter
- Needle tool
- Polyester fiberfill
- Paintbrush
- Paper towel
- Water-based acrylic floor polish

MAKING THE MIXES

Divide a 2 oz (56 g) block of pearl clay into eight. Mix one ball of pearl clay with one ⅛" (3 mm) ball of each of the colors and reserve the rest of the pearl clay for plain pearl sheets.

ROLLING THE CLAY

Roll the tinted and pearl sheets thinly using a roller or on the thinnest setting on a pasta machine, and tear into squares. Lay these out neatly. Stack the sheets, alternating the pearl and colored sheets.

CUTTING SLIVERS

Press the stack down so it sticks to the work surface and cannot slide around. Hold a very sharp tissue blade firmly with both hands and bend it to cut slivers from the top of the stack.

FINISHING THE SLICES

To make your slivers go farther, lay them on a sheet of medium thick, plain pearl clay, overlapping the edges. Use a roller or a pasta machine to gradually reduce the clay to a medium thickness. Turn the clay by 90° each time you roll.

MAKING THE STACK

Cut the stack in half with a tissue blade and place one stack on top of the other.

ADDING INTEREST TO THE LAYERS

With the palm of your hand, press down on the clay to bond all the layers. Make indentations in the top of the clay stack with the end of a paintbrush handle. Turn the stack over and make more indentations—this distorts the interior of the stack.

EXPELLING AIR POCKETS

Compress the stack from all sides with your fingers to exclude any air pockets and to further distort the layers inside the stack. Keep the stack in a rectangular shape.

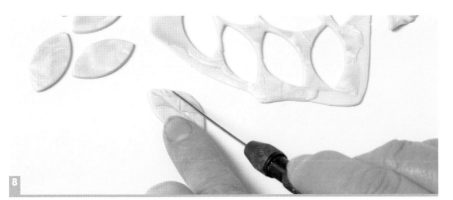

MAKING THE LEAF SHAPES

Cut out leaf shapes with a cookie cutter or sharp knife. Use a needle tool to draw on leaf veins and to make the serrated edges of the leaves. Make a thread hole with the needle tool. Slightly bend the leaf beads for a natural look and bake on a piece of polyester fiberfill (see page 17). Leave to cool. Apply a brown acrylic paint very sparingly with a paintbrush to "age" the beads. Wipe the paint off almost immediately with a paper towel before the paint dries. Lightly apply water-based acrylic floor polish to give the leaves a slight sheen.

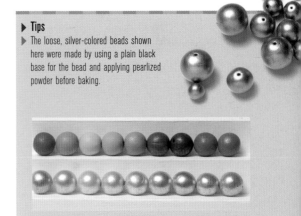

▶ **Tips**

▶ The loose, silver-colored beads shown here were made by using a plain black base for the bead and applying pearlized powder before baking.

▶ Interesting effects can also be achieved by making "pearls," using different colors for the base clay, and then using a pearlized powder before baking.

▶ **SEE ALSO**   ▶ Using a pasta machine, page 14   ▶ Baking, page 17   ▶ Cutting and slicing, page 28   ▶ Caning and stacking, page 30

A necklace of small disks, bicones, and oval beads wrapped with a thin extruded clay and finished with a silver powder *(left)*.

A necklace of faux silver beads decorated with thinly extruded clay and mixed with faux silver disks and melon shaped beads *(right)*.

SILVER

SILVER AND GOLD ARE THE PRIMARY metals used in jewelry. Both are soft and malleable, which make them ideal metals for beads, but silver remains the more commonly used for the robust ethnic styles that suit polymer clay. Balinese silver can have a dark patina in crevices where tarnish has accumulated between its intricate wire patterns. Here, a lighter version of the Balinese silver technique has been used, but the beads could be antiqued after baking with black or raw umber acrylic paint.

Ready-mixed silver clay looks more like gray dough than metal, so applying a pearlized powdered pigment provides a more realistic-looking silver finish. A light or white base color provides a good foundation for coating with silver powder, but you could use scrap clay or try the effect of a colored base. (See the string of pearls on page 89 to see how a different base color can alter the final appearance of powder coatings.)

TOOLS & MATERIALS
- White polymer clay
- Silver powder
- Bead roller
- Needle tool
- Extruder clay gun and small round disk
- Dust mask
- Soft brush
- Polyester fiberfill
- Water-based acrylic floor polish

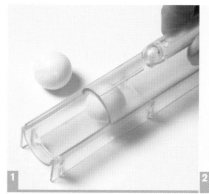

1 ROLLING THE CLAY BEADS
Roll a ball of white clay about ¾" (19 mm) in diameter. (If you need several beads all the same size, a bead roller is a good investment.)

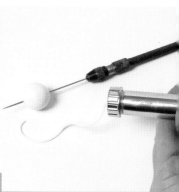

2 USING THE EXTRUDER TOOL
Pierce the ball through the center with the needle tool. Shape enough clay to fit the extruder clay gun barrel and extrude a long string of clay.

6 ADDING THE SILVER EFFECT
Put on a dust mask. Using a dry brush, dust the unbaked clay with the silver powder, over a piece of paper. Brush off the excess powder. Bake the bead on polyester fiberfill (see page 17). When the bead is cool, apply one coat of water-based acrylic floor polish to seal the silver powder.

▶ **Tip**
▶ After varnishing the bead, you could "antique" it by applying black or raw umber acrylic paint to the crevices, then wiping off the excess with a paper towel before it has dried.

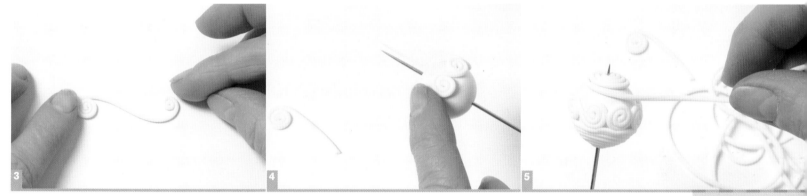

MAKING A SPIRAL

Cut a 4" (100 mm) length from the string of clay and make a spiral at each end. Repeat to make two more double spirals.

ADDING THE SPIRALS

Position the three double spirals around the middle of the bead.

EMBELLISHING THE BEAD

Use a long piece of extruded clay to make a spiral that starts at the thread hole (see tip, right) and wind down the bead.

▶ **Tip**

▶ To make it easier to embellish the bead, make a few turns of the spiral away from the bead on the work surface, then thread it onto the needle tool and work down onto the bead.

HOLLOW BEADS

This technique produces light, hollow beads, patterned with holes and craters.

TOOLS & MATERIALS

- White polymer clay
- Silver powder
- Escargot serving tray
- Cookie cutters
- Ball stylus
- Water-based acrylic floor polish
- Sandpaper
- Superglue

MARKING THE CLAY

Tear pieces of medium-thick clay for each dome of the escargot serving tray. Cut small, decorative circles but do not remove the pieces at this stage. Make marks in the clay with a ball stylus.

REMOVING THE WASTE

Use a large cookie cutter to cut a circle and remove the waste and the small, cut circles.

BAKING THE PIECES

Apply the silver powder and bake the pieces.

Each bead was made of two pieces sanded and joined with superglue, then fitted with an eye pin for hanging. The beads were given a light coat of protective varnish.

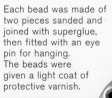

▶ **SEE ALSO** ▶ Baking, page 17 ▶ Bead shapes, page 38 ▶ Varnishing, page 49

A necklace of tube beads made from pieces of malachite cane.

MALACHITE

MALACHITE, A COPPER MINERAL WITH CONCENTRIC growth rings, forms in the spaces between other rocks. It was highly prized in Imperial Russia as a veneer for precious objects as well as jewelry. Today, most malachite beads come from central Africa.

Jewelers slice through a block of malachite to reveal bands of light and dark green that reflect the changing conditions under which the mineral was deposited over many centuries. Polymer clay imitations are more convincing if there is variation in both the size of the circles and the sequence of the bands.

TOOLS & MATERIALS
- Polymer clay—turquoise, tropical or bright green, mid blue, black, and white
- Tissue blade
- Roller or pasta machine
- Thin knitting needle

▶ **Tip**
▶ Cut the cane in half and stack the two halves with opposite ends side by side. This immediately doubles the size of the cane but also shortens it.

MAKING THE MIXES

Mix the clay: (A) Three parts turquoise to two parts tropical green and one part blue—reserve a third of the mix and use the rest for the other mixes; (B) four parts A to one part black; (C) eight parts A to one part black; (D) two parts A to one part white; (E) one part A to one part white.

ROLLING THE CLAY

Using your hands, roll ½" (13 mm) thick logs of the B and E mixes and trim the ends with a tissue blade to make each log 3" (75 mm) long. Use a roller or pasta machine to roll out sheets of the other three mixes. Vary the thickness of the sheets.

TIDYING THE CANE

Use a knitting needle to press the sheet into the grooves.

FINISHING THE CANE

Continue to bundle and add more logs. Wrap them in a final sheet of polymer clay and hide the join in a groove. The malachite cane can now be sliced to make flat beads or cut up for chunkier beads.

Flat, oval beads, cut from a thick slice of faux malachite and sanded to round the edges. A black coil bead is attached to each for threading the cord through.

Arrowhead beads in extruded faux malachite clay, cut with a cookie cutter and bordered with black clay.

WRAPPING THE LOGS

Cut one of the lighter sheets of clay to 3" (75 mm). Wrap the dark B log in the sheet and cut the sheet so that the long edges butt together. Repeat with a dark sheet and the light E log.

REDUCING LOGS TO MAKE THE CANE

Wrap more contrasting sheets around each of the logs. Roll each log until it is about 6" (150 mm) long. Cut in half with a tissue blade and set one half aside. Hand roll the remaining half to twice its original length, halve again, and set one half aside.

BUNDLING THE LOGS

Roll out the remaining half to twice its length and halve again. Do this once more. You should now have logs in four different diameters, all about 3" (75 mm) long. Bundle together a few logs of different sizes and wrap with a sheet of clay.

EXTRUDED MALACHITE

Using an extruder clay gun quickly makes a faux malachite. Although the malachite is on a smaller scale than is usually found in nature, it is, nonetheless, ideal for delicate bead projects.

MIXING THE CLAY

Mix a variety of colored clays. Roll to a medium thickness using a roller or a pasta machine, then roll half of each color on a thin setting.

CUTTING OUT THE SHAPES

Use the cookie cutter to cut disks from each sheet and randomly stack them.

USING THE EXTRUDER

Compress the stack and roll it until it fits into the extruder barrel. Extrude several lengths of clay.

TOOLS & MATERIALS

● Use the same clay mixes and tools as for the main malachite recipe (see opposite). You will also need an extruder clay gun with a large-hole die, and a small circular cookie cutter measuring ⅝" (15 mm) in diameter, or slightly smaller than the barrel of your clay gun.

FORMING A CANE

Lay the small extruded clay canes together, rolling them out to make them longer if any are too short.

BUNDLING UP THE CANES

Wrap a thin sheet of clay around the bundle, and press it into the grooves with a knitting needle.

THE COMPLETED CANE

Fill gaps with snakes of clay. Wrap a clay sheet around the entire cane and bury the end in a groove.

▶ SEE ALSO ▶ Using a pasta machine, page 14 ▶ Baking, page 17 ▶ Cutting and slicing, page 28 ▶ Caning and stacking, page 30 ▶ Extrusions, page 50

A pendant necklace threaded with irregular-shaped nuggets of American southwestern-style turquoise, pieces of faux coral, and silver beads.

TURQUOISE

TURQUOISE IS A MINERAL FOUND in many parts of the world, and while each region has its own distinctive colors, textures, and patterns, there are also numerous variations. It seems that no two pieces of turquoise are ever quite the same. Fortunately, this leaves much scope for polymer clayers to experiment with color and textures. Therefore, don't worry about being too precise with the color mixes as subtle differences between beads that are strung side by side make them look more real.

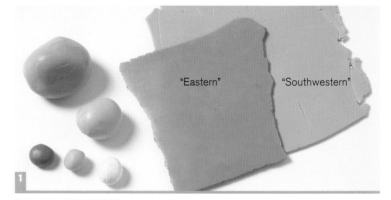

"Eastern"   "Southwestern"

MAKING THE MIXES

There are two basic turquoise mixes. For eastern-style turquoise, the base mix is ten parts turquoise clay to one part each of caramel and yellow. For some of the beads, vary the proportions of the colors for a more realistic turquoise, as found in nature. For a lighter look, with a flavor of the southwestern United States, make a base mix with eight parts turquoise to one part each of white and ecru.

TOOLS & MATERIALS
- Polymer clay—turquoise, caramel, sunflower-yellow, ecru, and white
- Scrap clay (optional)
- Black acrylic paint
- Roller or pasta machine
- Ripple blade
- Needle tool
- 400–800-grit wet and dry sandpapers
- Cotton cloth for buffing
- Water-based acrylic floor polish
- Grater
- Polyester fiberfill
  - Stiff paintbrush
  - Paper towel

Earrings made with eastern faux turquoise.

PAINTING THE CLAY

Cover all the pieces of clay with undiluted black acrylic paint, straight from the tube. Leave to dry.

MAKING THE BEAD CENTER

Form a bead core of similar colored scrap clay. Press on the painted chunks. Shape the beads in your hands, varying the shape of each bead. Using a needle tool, make a thread hole, or drill the hole after baking. Bake the bead (see page 17).

Eastern turquoise beads with faux coral tube beads and gold metal round beads.

CHOPPING THE CLAY

Mix the "eastern" base clays together. (If you used a pasta machine to mix the colors, roll up the sheets into a choppable lump.) Use a ripple blade to chop the clay as this gives more rounded lumps than a straight tissue blade. Vary the size of the chunks: some small, some large.

SANDING AND BUFFING

When cool, use 400–800-grit sandpapers and wet-sand to remove the outer paint layer and reveal the black matrix found in old Indian and Tibetan beads. Buff the bead with a cotton cloth or apply a coat of water-based acrylic floor polish.

SOUTHWESTERN TURQUOISE

Use the lighter clay mix, and a slightly different technique for adding "imperfections," to achieve the look of turquoise from the American southwest.

Earrings made with American faux turquoise, faux coral, and silver beads.

CHOPPING THE CLAY

Mix the "southwestern" base clays together. Chop up the clay with a ripple blade to make rounded shapes. Vary the size of the chunks.

▶ **Tip**
▶ Roll your fingertips or the palm of your hand over the chopped bits to round the pieces more. Or use a food processor to cut the clay pieces as this makes them more round.

FORMING THE BEAD SHAPE

Mold the bits of clay to make nugget-sized beads and pierce a hole for the thread using a needle tool.

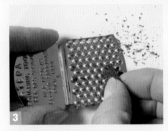

GRATING THE CLAY

Finely grate some baked dark brown or black clay.

APPLYING THE GRATINGS

Lightly press the raw clay bead into the gratings to simulate natural imperfections. Don't add too much or you will overdo it. Bake the beads on polyester fiberfill (see page 17) and allow to cool.

PAINTING THE BEAD

With a paintbrush, paint and stipple black acrylic paint into the crevices of the bead. Almost immediately wipe off the excess paint with a paper towel. Buff the bead with a cotton cloth or apply a coat of water-based acrylic floor polish.

▶ **SEE ALSO** ▶ *Baking, page 17* ▶ *Sanding and polishing, page 48*

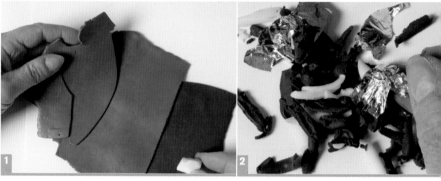

A multistranded necklace of small tube beads of lapis lazuli threaded with gold charms and small gold beads *(right)*, and matching earrings *(left)*.

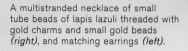

LAPIS LAZULI

LAPIS LAZULI IS A RARE BLUE stone made up of several minerals that can alter its color from intense ultramarine to pale blue. The best quality comes from Afghanistan and has long been used as beads to protect the wearer from evil; it's even featured in the mask of Tutankhamen. The beads are often quite small and exhibit a variety of blues with inclusions of translucent calcite and flecks of gold pyrite.

The secret of a successful lapis lazuli imitation is to not over-mix the ingredients, but to ensure that they are mixed well enough to present an even, fine grain structure with only random calcite (translucent polymer clay) and gold flecks clearly visible.

TOOLS & MATERIALS
- Polymer clay—ultramarine, mid blue, black, white, pearl, and translucent
- Grater
- Gold crafter's metal foil
- Tissue blade
- A straight piece of wire for rolling the beads on
- Polyester fiberfill
- Water-based acrylic floor polish

1

MIXING THE CLAY

Make a base mix of equal parts of ultramarine and mid-blue. Divide the mix into three portions. Use one part black clay to thirty parts base mix in the first portion; one part white clay to ten parts base mix in the second; and one part pearl clay to ten parts base mix in the third portion.

2

ADDING FOIL

Take one of the blue mixes and a piece of translucent clay in proportions of four parts blue to one part translucent. Using a grater, coarsely grate the clays together and press pieces of gold crafter's foil onto the clay. Push the mix together.

6

ROLLING THE BEADS

Roll out small amounts of clay to make into tube beads or flat beads as used in the memory wire bracelet (opposite).

7

MAKING TUBE BEADS

To make tube beads, prepare a ¾" (19 mm) ball of clay and push it onto a stiff piece of straight wire (you will need several lengths of wire to bake a mass of beads at once).

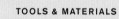

GRATING THE CLAY

With the coarse side of a grater, grate the clay; or with a tissue blade finely chop the clay.

FINE GRATING

Press the bits together and grate again for a finer grained look.

GRATING THE OTHER MIXES

Repeat Steps 2 to 4 with the remaining two blue mixes.

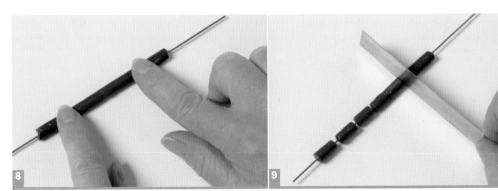

ROLLING THE TUBES

With the wire horizontal to a smooth work surface, roll the pierced ball of clay back and forth into a log. Use your fingertips to keep reducing the diameter of the log as it expands widthways to cover more of the wire. Stop when the log—now a snake—is about ¼" (6 mm) in diameter.

BAKING AND FINISHING THE BEADS

While the snake is still on the wire, cut it into short ¼"–¾" (6–18 mm) lengths with a tissue blade. Gently move the beads apart along the wire. Support the wire in a baking tray so the beads don't rest on the tray. Alternatively, beads can be unthreaded from the wire and baked on polyester fiberfill.

A bracelet of lapis lazuli beads with gold charms threaded onto a spiral of memory wire.

Bake (see page 17) then leave to cool. When cool, seal with water-based acrylic floor polish to prevent the gold foil from tarnishing.

▶ **SEE ALSO**   ▶ *Using a pasta machine, page 14*   ▶ *Baking, page 17*   ▶ *Making logs and sheets, page 18*

A necklace of sanded and polished faux onyx beads.

ONYX

ONYX IS A MINERAL WITH COLORED IMPURITIES, which form banded deposits. Onyx bands are quite straight, suiting more block-shaped beads. There is much scope for varying the mixtures and colors but keep a high proportion of translucent clay in each mix as this lends a very convincing glassy depth to a polished bead. Polymer clay onyx (and agate, see page 100) beads are lighter and warmer to the touch than real stone beads. If you make onyx beads individually as shown, you can experiment with varying the order of their bands.

The mixed sheets (from the left of the picture).

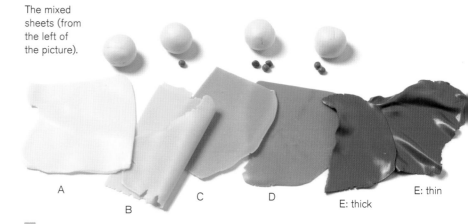

A

B

C

D

E: thick

E: thin

1 MAKING THE MIXES

Divide a 2 oz (56 g) block of translucent clay into four 1" (25 mm) balls. Roll five ¼" (6 mm) balls of caramel and one ¼" (6 mm) ball of copper for mixing. Mix the sheets as follows: (A) translucent with no additions; (B) translucent with one ball caramel; (C) translucent with three balls caramel; (D) translucent with one ball caramel and one ball copper; (E) one part caramel with one part copper.

Roll out the sheets with a pasta machine as follows:
A: thickest setting
B: thin (setting 5)
C: thin (setting 5)
D: medium thickness (setting 4)
E: roll half a sheet on medium thickness, and half on thinnest (setting 6).

TOOLS & MATERIALS
- Polymer clay—translucent, caramel, and copper mica
- White acrylic paint
- Pasta machine
- Piece of glass or a tile
- Cherry or orange stick
- Liquid polymer clay
- Paintbrush
- Round ½" (13 mm) cookie cutter
- Needle tool
- Wire skewer
- 240–800-grit wet and dry sandpapers
- Buffing machine or a piece of denim

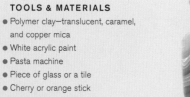

A pair of faux onyx earrings.

Order of stacking

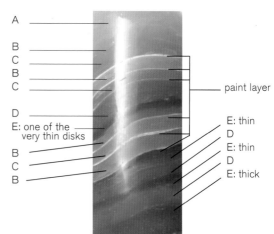

A

B
C
B
C

paint layer

D

E: one of the very thin disks

B
C
B

E: thin
D
E: thin
D
E: thick

Teardrop-shaped beads made from a different arrangement of colored layers.

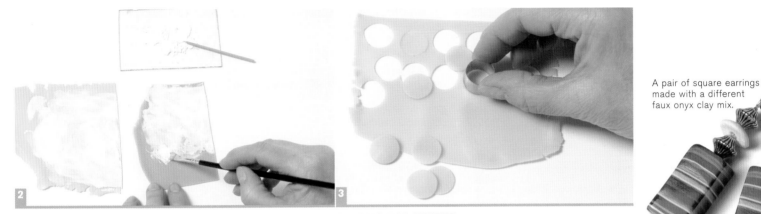

A pair of square earrings made with a different faux onyx clay mix.

PAINTING THE SHEETS

On a piece of glass or tile, use a cherry stick to mix equal amounts of white acrylic paint and liquid polymer clay. With a paintbrush, brush sheets B and C with the paint mix and leave to dry.

CUTTING THE SHAPES

Use the cookie cutter to cut out a lot of disks from all the sheets of clay.

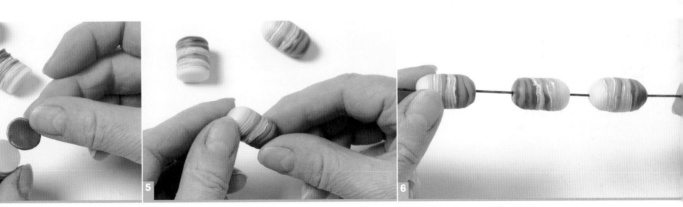

STACKING THE DISKS

Stack the disks in the order shown on the left. For some of the beads, try varying the order of layers or starting at a different number in the list.

SHAPING THE BEADS

Use your fingers to shape the ends of the bead. Make the thread hole through the bead with the needle tool.

BAKING THE BEADS

Place the beads on a straight wire and bake supported in the oven (see page 17). When the beads are cool, wet-sand them using 240–800-grit sandpaper. Use a buffing machine for a final high polish if that is the look you want, or use a piece of denim to give your beads a satin-sheen finish.

▶ **SEE ALSO** ▶ Using a pasta machine, page 14 ▶ Baking, page 17 ▶ Caning and stacking, page 30 ▶ Sanding and polishing, page 48

A necklace of beads made of cut slices of faux agate, linked with jump rings to a silver chain.

AGATE

AGATE IS FORMED FROM THE SAME MINERAL AS ONYX. It tends to have concentric bands and is cut into slices to emphasize its translucency. For the faux onyx beads (see page 98) and the agate beads, the same colors and order of colored layers have been used. However, just as in nature, the different way that onyx and agate are made and cut results in an entirely different appearance. For onyx, disks are stacked, but for agate, a cane is built up by wrapping colored sheets of varying thickness around a log of translucent clay.

TOOLS AND MATERIALS
- Polymer clay—translucent, caramel, and copper mica
- White acrylic paint
- Pasta machine
- Piece of glass or a tile
- Cherry or orange stick
- Liquid polymer clay
- Cotton swab
- Stiff plastic credit card or similar
- Tissue blade
- 400–800-grit wet and dry sandpapers
- Buffing machine or a piece of denim

▶ **Tip**
▶ For a gloss finish, bake the slices on a smooth tile or glass sheet.

1 MAKING THE MIXES

Divide a 2 oz (56 g) block of translucent clay into four 1" (25 mm) balls. Roll ¼" (6 mm) balls of caramel and copper for mixing. Mix the sheets as follows: (A) translucent with no additions; (B) translucent with one ball caramel; (C) translucent with three balls caramel; (D) translucent with one ball caramel and one ball copper; (E) one part caramel to one part copper.

Roll out the sheets with a pasta machine as follows:
A: thickest setting
B: thin (setting 5)
C: thin (setting 5)
D: medium thickness (setting 4)
E: roll half a sheet on medium thickness and half on thinnest (setting 6).

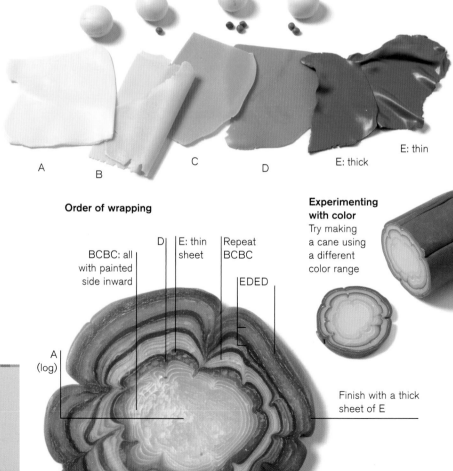

A   B   C   D   E: thick   E: thin

Order of wrapping

A (log)
BCBC: all with painted side inward
D | E: thin sheet | Repeat BCBC
EDED

Experimenting with color
Try making a cane using a different color range

Finish with a thick sheet of E

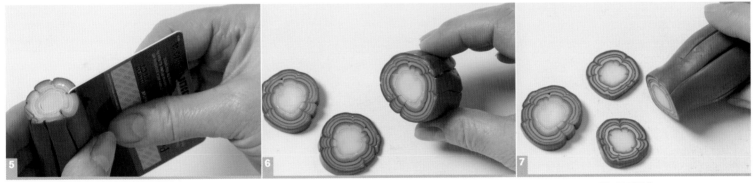

PAINTING THE SHEETS

Cut sheets B and C so they are 3" (75 mm) wide. On a piece of glass or a tile, use a cherry stick to mix equal amounts of white acrylic paint and liquid polymer clay. Using a cotton swab, paint the mixture onto one side of the B and C sheets. Leave to dry.

WRAPPING THE LOG

Roll sheet A into a log about ½ x 3" (13 x 75 mm) long and wrap it in the painted sheet B. Butt the joins together. Wrap a painted sheet of C around the log. Wrap another sheet of B and then another sheet of C around the log. (You should now have four painted sheets covering the translucent log.)

WRAPPING THE CANE

Wrap the cane in a sheet of D and butt the edges together. Wrap with a very thin sheet of E.

INDENTING THE CANE

Make indentations along the full length of the cane. A stiff plastic credit card works well, forcing the bands of clay into each other.

THE CANE

Continue to wrap the indented cane with sheet B, then C, then B, then C, then thin E, then D, then thin E, then D, ending with a thick sheet of E. Make more indentations as before using a credit card. Check the appearance at both ends of the cane. Cut into slices with a tissue blade.

MAKING SMALLER SLICES

If you want some smaller slices, then reduce the cane by squeezing with your fingers at one end. Bake the slices (see page 17) and let cool. Wet-sand using 400–800-grit sandpapers. Use a buffing machine for a high polish or a piece of denim for a satin sheen finish.

▶ **SEE ALSO** ▶ *Using a pasta machine, page 14* ▶ *Baking, page 17* ▶ *Making logs and sheets, page 18* ▶ *Caning and stacking, page 30*

SECTION THREE

BRINGING IT

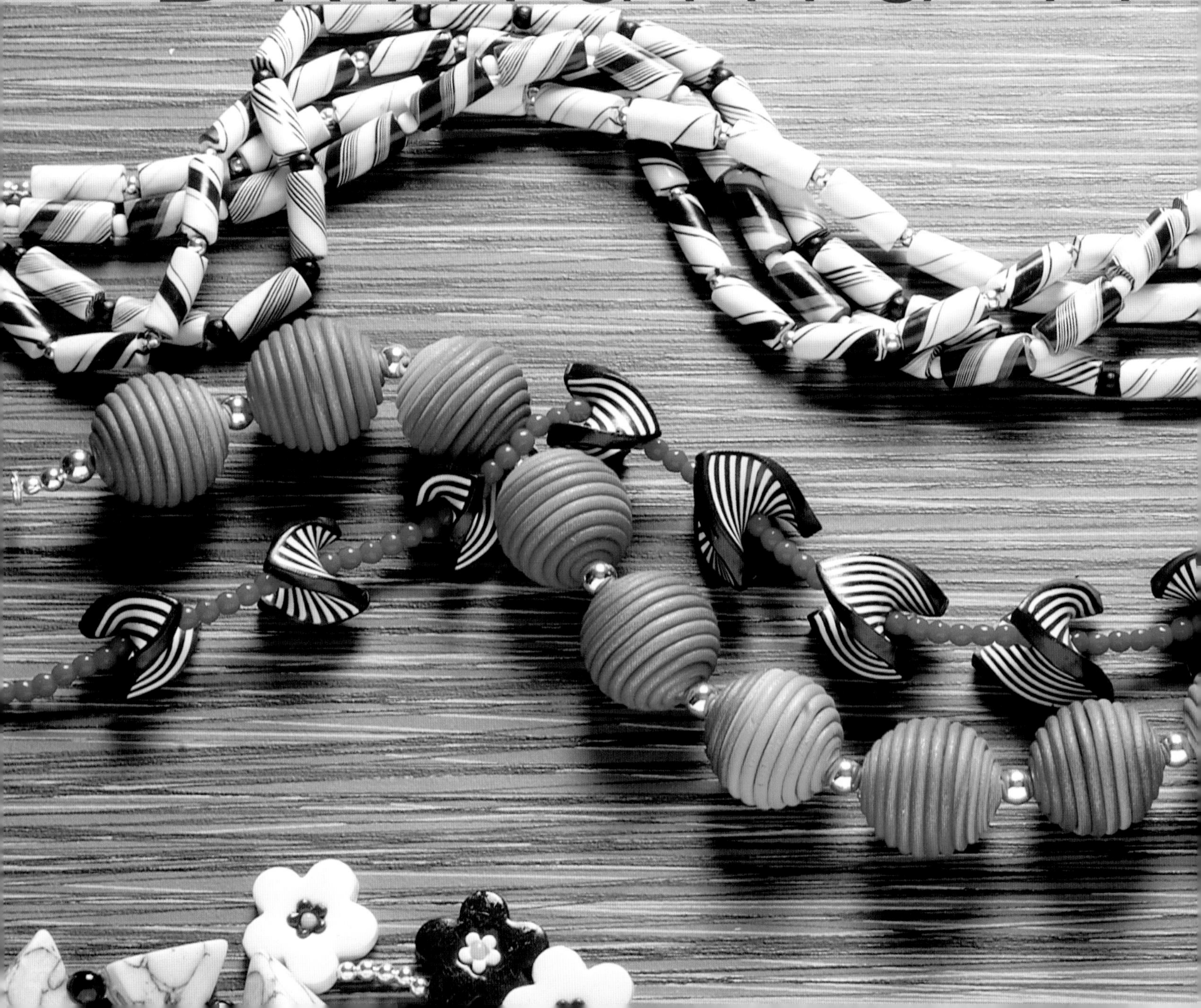

ALL TOGETHER

FINDINGS AND THREADS

Findings are small metal components that are used to complete a piece of jewelry and can be decorative as well as functional. Findings can be made from nonprecious base metal, which is then either plated with or dipped in a nickel, silver, or gold solution. You can purchase more expensive findings made using gold or sterling silver. If you have concerns about nickel allergy reactions, buy findings that are labeled "nickel allergy free" or "hypoallergenic."

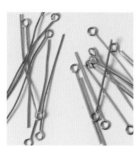

EYE PINS

Eye pins have a loop of wire at one end and are used for attaching beads and charms to a chain.

HEAD PINS

Head pins are straight wires up to 3" (75 mm) long, with a flattened end to keep the beads from falling off. They are used for beaded earrings that are designed to dangle.

KNOT CUPS

Knot cups are tiny, hinged, clam-shaped cups with a small metal loop, and are used to hide and hold the knots of the beading thread at the ends of a necklace.

SPRING-END CRIMPS

Spring-end crimps are used with thonging, such as leather or rubber cord to attach the thong to the fastener.

JUMP RINGS

Jump rings are used to connect findings, such as a fastener, to a knot cup. They are also used for attaching disk beads to other disk beads or a bead or charm to a chain.

SPLIT RINGS

Like key rings with double rings of wire, split rings are stronger and more secure than jump rings. They are difficult to open unless you use a pair of split-ring pliers.

Half of this slide clasp *(below)* is concealed in a round bead. When closed, the clasp on the necklace is nearly invisible.

A screw clasp embedded in two half-beads *(right)*. When the clasp is closed, the "bead" conceals it completely.

STUDS AND HOOPS

Earstuds have a flat pad for gluing beads or cabachons onto for pierced ears. Earhoops can vary from small hoops, as shown, up to 3" (76 mm) in diameter, onto which beads can be threaded.

FISHHOOK WIRES

Fishhook wires hook through the pierced ear. The loop is opened like a jump ring to hook onto the beadwork. The bead and coil are decorative.

KIDNEY WIRES

Made from one piece of wire, kidney wires pass through the pierced ear and are secured by a hook on the other end of the wire.

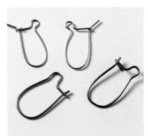

BOLT OR SPRING RING

Bolt or spring rings have a sliding section that springs closed when a lever is released. The slide may be stiff to open or fail to close. Check this before fitting one to your necklace.

LOBSTER CLAW CLASPS

Lobster claw or trigger clasps have a hinged bar that is operated with a spring lever to keep it closed.

TOGGLES

Toggle or ring-and-bar clasps are available in a wide choice of styles, sizes, and weights. The T-bar must be able to pass through the ring, turn, and lie flat.

HOOK AND EYE

With hook-and-eye fasteners the hook is not closed, so they are best used where the weight of the beads holds the fastener taut.

MAGNETIC CLASPS

Magnetic clasps are useful for people with arthritis, but they are not as readily available as other fasteners.

SCREW CLASPS

Screw clasps screw shut and are available with or without a loop.

A toggle closure *(left)*—both beads made using the same decorative clay.

A toggle closure using two beads from the same family *(left)*. The looped rubber cord captures the toggle bead and is pulled tight.

CORDS AND THREADS

Match the actual and visual weight of the beads with the thickness and strength of the stringing thread. If you use a fine thread and heavy beads, it may stretch and show at the clasp.

THREAD HOLES

The size of the thread hole limits the size of the thread, for example, nylon thread will fit through a small hole, while rubber cord will require a larger hole. Sometimes the thread hole can be enlarged a little using a reamer tool, but for greater enlarging use a drill and bit (see page 48).

Thread holes can be made in different positions on a bead, but remember that the position of the thread hole will affect how the bead hangs.

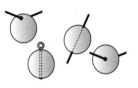

Lentil beads can be threaded in several ways or hung from an eye pin.

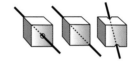

Cubes can be threaded through the center, corner to corner, or edge to edge.

Macaroni beads are tubes and are easy to thread—or alternatively, pierce them across the tube.

A teardrop can take a simple thread hole, a glued-in eye pin, or a jump ring to vary the way it hangs.

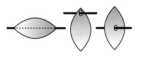

Oval or lozenge beads can be threaded lengthwise, through one end, or through the center

A cone bead can be threaded from top to bottom, through the tip of the cone, or take a glued-in eye pin.

NYLON

Nylon comes in several thicknesses, with different breaking strengths. Choose the right thickness for the size bead you are threading.

CHAINS

Chains come in different designs and are used for bracelets and necklaces. You can attach beads or charms to chains using jump rings.

RATTAIL

Rattail is a silky cord with a hidden core of cotton and comes in a wide range of colors, as in knotted rattail (see page 112).

RUBBER CORD

Rubber cord is usually black, but can be obtained in a few other colors as well as various thicknesses.

ELASTIC THREAD

Elastic thread is good for stretchy bracelets. It is available in many thicknesses and comes in black, clear, and an assortment of colors.

MEMORY WIRE

Memory wire is a flexible coiled wire, which springs back to its original shape each time it is stretched and released. It is made of hardened steel and comes in various sizes.

LEATHER THONG

Leather thong is ideal for large beads with large holes.

WAXED COTTON CORD

Waxed cotton cord is a good alternative to leather.

SHOELACES

Cotton or linen shoelaces can be used to string beads.

NECK RINGS

Neck rings are ready-made rings for beads and pendants, as in the faux jade teardrop beads (see page 87).

READY-MADE

Ready-made necklaces fitted with closures and findings for hanging a single pendant bead

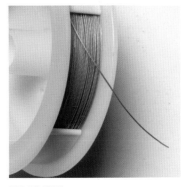

TIGER TAIL

Tiger tail is a thin, tightly twisted strand of wire, which is coated in clear nylon.

ATTACHING FINDINGS

A finding must be correctly fitted and attached properly. Too small a clasp on a necklace of heavy beads may not be strong enough to take the weight, but too large a clasp on a string of delicate beads can look clumsy. Practice using your tools to attach jump rings, fit knot cups, and cleanly cut and bend wires into neat loops to make a secure closure.

▶ **Tip**
▶ Use a reamer—a tapered metal shaft with an abrasive coating—or a needle file, to enlarge thread holes in baked beads. If you need to enlarge the hole more, you will need to use a drill and drill bit (see page 48).

PLIERS

There are a variety of pliers, each suited to specific findings.

ROUND-NOSE PLIERS

Round-nose pliers are used for forming round loops in wire.

FLAT-NOSE PLIERS

Flat-nose pliers have round tips and are flat on the inside. They can be used to open jump rings, squeeze crimps, and make loops.

WIRE CUTTERS

Wire cutters are essential for cutting head- and eyepin wires. Buy a pair with neat, pointed ends to cut close to the work. To cut memory wire you will need a pair of heavy duty cutters.

COIL PLIERS

Coil pliers are specialist pliers designed for making identical loops in any of three sizes.

SPLIT-RING PLIERS

Split-ring pliers are useful for opening split rings, as they have a hook on one end that will hold the ring open while you add your bead or attach to another finding—something that is challenging to do any other way.

ATTACHING A KNOT CUP

Many beaded necklaces are threaded with cords that need to be knotted and attached to a fastener.

OPENING THE KNOT CUP LOOP

Open the loop of the knot cup with the pliers by gently twisting the loop to one side. Insert a split ring, then close the loop again with the pliers.

CLOSING THE KNOT CUP

Tie a knot in the beading thread (leaving a short end), and place the knot into the cupped section of the knot cup. Use the pliers to squeeze the knot cup closed over the knot; there is a small groove for the thread to pass out of. Cut the free end of the thread close to the knot cup.

ATTACHING A JUMP RING

Jump rings are small metal rings that are not fully joined together. They are used to link components together easily. Opening jump rings sideways avoids distorting the rings.

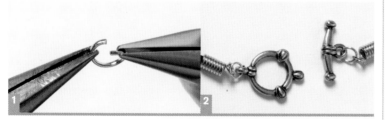

ATTACHING A JUMP RING

Open the jump ring by twisting the ends sideways, away from each other, using two pairs of pliers—one in each hand. Attach a component, then close the ring by twisting the ends back toward each other until the ends are even.

ASSEMBLED FINDINGS

The ends of a rubber cord have been secured in spring-end crimps and attached to a toggle with jump rings.

SPRING-END CRIMPS

When using thicker cord or thong, the ends can be finished and held securely with spring-end crimps.

ATTACHING THE CRIMP

Cut the end of the cord or thong and insert it into the crimp. Squeeze the end of the crimp with pliers to crimp the metal onto the cord. Use a jump ring or spring ring to attach a clasp to the spring-end crimp.

ATTACHING A HEAD PIN

A drop earring made with a head pin and fishhook ear wire is ideal for displaying feature beads.

ADDING THE BEADS

Thread the beads onto a straight head pin, leaving one end of the wire exposed.

TRIMMING THE WIRE

Bend the end of the wire 90°. Cut the wire with the wire cutters, leaving about ⅜" (9 mm) or enough to make a loop.

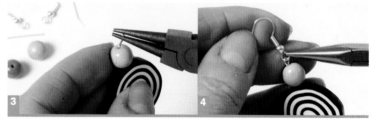

MAKING A LOOP

Using the round-nose pliers, grasp the end of the wire and turn the pliers to form a loop. Check that the loop is centered over the beads.

ATTACHING THE EAR WIRE

Slightly open the loop on the fishhook ear wire by twisting it to one side with the flat-nose pliers. Attach the looped head pin and close the loop.

DESIGNING WITH BEADS

YOU HAVE FINISHED MAKING YOUR BEADS and are ready to string them together. You may have already planned how to use your beads, or you may be waiting for inspiration. Lay your beads out and see if your idea works or what the beads may be best suited to: necklaces, bracelets, earrings, brooches, or even bead embellishments on belts, bags, key fobs, or light pulls. At each step in the design process (whether stringing, deciding on length, or choosing spacer beads) ask yourself, "What if I did it differently?" Experiment to see what looks best and remember you can always unstring the beads and start again.

> ▶ **Tip**
> ▶ Before you unstring a bead arrangement to try a new version, take a photo in case you realize you prefer the first arrangement and want to remember how to remake it.

Long strands of beads can be worn in many ways.

BEAD BOARD

Use a bead board to lay your beads out on so that they don't roll around. This useful tray of molded plastic has three grooves, compartments for holding beads, and printed measurements, making designing easier as you try different arrangements of beads.

SIZE

If the necklace is more than 24" (600 mm) long, and is large enough to fit over the head without a closure fitting, there is no need to add one. However, adding a closure to a long necklace means the necklace can be worn wrapped two or more times around the neck.

TEXTURE

The natural matt finish of polymer clay gives a unique look to polymer clay beads. Make the most of textures by contrasting rough with smooth, metal with clay, large with small.

Swirling colors and writhing shapes combine to make strong knotted textures.

SHAPE

Sharp, angular shapes call for attention and are perfect for striking, glitzy necklaces, whereas soft, round shapes are more conservative. Put round beads between tube beads and larger beads to act as ball joints that help the necklace to flow smoothly.

Smooth oval beads are strung together with matt clay disks and tube beads impressed with a crackle texture.

This necklace is long and flexible enough to be wound into a multistrand bracelet.

COLOR

In time you will develop your own distinctive color palette for your designs, but in the meantime enjoy the fact that polymer clay beads can be made in colors and patterns that match or complement any outfit.

Purple/blue accent

Green/gold accent

Brown/tan accent

Three necklaces, all using swirl beads, show a variety of color options. The subtle, monochromatic range from black to gray to white has been accented with different colors.

Simple color combinations can create strong dynamic contrasts.

Harmonious colors such as blues, turquoises, and greens work well together.

The bold use of bright primary colors with black and white can be very effective.

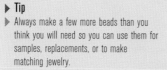

▶ **Tip**
▶ Always make a few more beads than you think you will need so you can use them for samples, replacements, or to make matching jewelry.

WEIGHT

Polymer clay is lighter than most other bead materials and can be made lighter still by using foil or Sculpey Ultra Light (see page 10) as a bead core. The weight of the beads will often determine the type of beading thread you use, as some threads such as nylon may stretch. Bear this in mind when choosing the thread.

Faux polymer coral combined with a mix of bead shapes in glass, metal, and natural materials such as shells and nuts.

COMBINING BEADS

Make full use of inexpensive, store-bought spacer beads. Spacers are used between polymer clay beads to provide contrasting shapes, colors, and textures, to fill space, and to add length to a finished necklace. Contrast a few large textured beads with many small plain spacer beads. Check out yard sales, thrift shops, and flea markets for old necklaces. The beads and clasps can be recycled, giving them a new life in your necklace.

SYMMETRICAL

Symmetrical patterns are the same each side of the center, the two halves mirroring each other. Symmetry is reinforced by gradually decreasing the size of the beads toward the closure. Precision is key, so try to make the bead hole exactly through the center of the bead. When the necklace is symmetrical, an off-balanced bead can be very distracting to the eye.

STYLE AND IDEAS

Keep a note of ideas you gain from your environment. Browse in shops for color ideas, look at fashion magazines for inspiration, and get ideas from what you see at the movies or on television. If designing for a specific person (or yourself), consider their style and character; a quiet reserved person won't be comfortable in a huge statement necklace, while a small, delicate necklace might be lost on a more extroverted dresser.

Clusters of striped tubes make a fresh, modern statement.

Pearly twist sticks are threaded with colored rattail cords that are knotted for a novel effect.

ASYMMETRICAL

Asymmetrical patterned necklaces use a feature bead threaded to lie to one side of the center. They can be balanced either by visual weight, texture, or color on the other side of the necklace.

Plain black beads focus attention on two swirl beads placed off-center in the necklace.

A range of different-sized beads are placed at angles by postioning the thread-hole in asymmetric positions.

RANDOM

Random arrangement can be fun as there are no hard-and-fast rules to follow. However, just stringing beads of any color or shape won't usually work unless you use beads that have some connection, and you make conscious decisions about their positioning on an appropriate cord. It can work for faux-aged beads that appear to have been collected and restrung over many decades.

Tube beads strung in no particular order retain unity by sharing similar shapes and colors.

A bracelet in a random mix of colors and shapes, threaded with stretch elastic.

REPEATING

Repeating patterns are those where a pattern of a set of beads is duplicated around the necklace. The necklace will be made up of groups of the pattern, and the ends of the necklace should have a complete pattern before attaching the clasp (see Vera beads, page 29).

Three Vera bead necklaces threaded in different repeated sequences; color can also be used as part of the repeat.

A limited palette of just two colors works to great effect when used in combination with beads of two different sizes.

Two effective ways of using a repeating color spectrum are shown in the necklaces below.

> ▶ **Tip**
> ▶ No matter how good the necklace looks when lying flat on the work surface, check that the beads also hang well around the neck.

SECTION FOUR

THE GALLERY

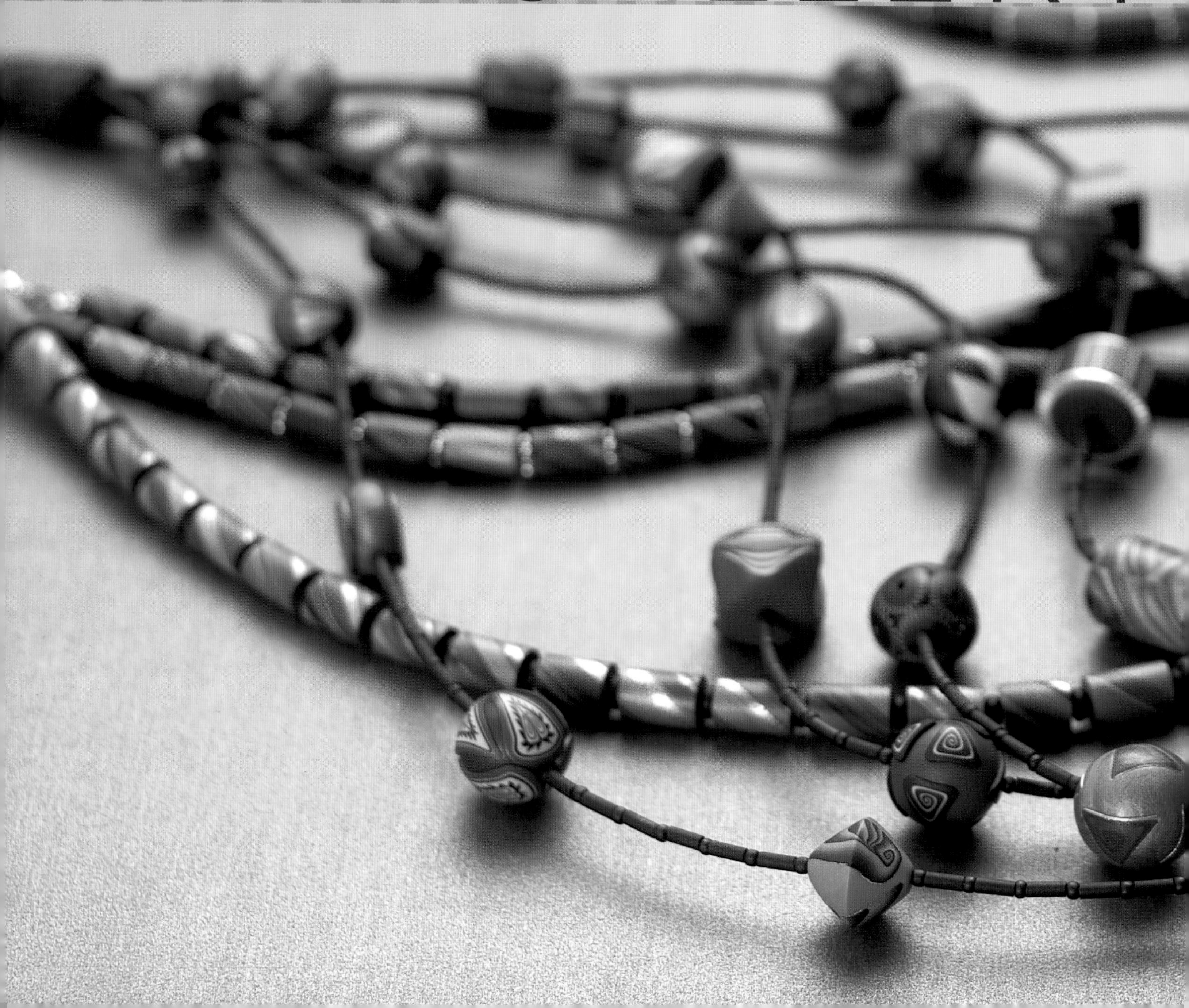

A selection of multistrand necklaces by Margaret Regan, showing a variety of bead shapes and techniques, including caning and inlay.

ELLIE HITCHCOCK
Nautilus Necklace

Skinner blends (see page 22) of gold mica and green polymer clay lend a sophisticated glitter to this necklace, which exploits texture and different thread-hole positions (see page 106) cleverly to build interest. The largest bead is 1½ " (38 mm) in diameter. The spacer beads are a mix of gold mica and green polymer clay—by twisting them the mica shift effect (see page 66) has been clearly revealed.
Private collection.

LYNNE ANN SCHWARZENBERG
Abacus

(Top left.) This necklace is made of inlaid ivory, turquoise, ebony, and coral, faux polymer clay beads (see pages 74, 80, and 94), patinated to achieve an antique appearance. The beads have been threaded onto silver head pins to form drop beads. Artist's collection.

DIANE VILLANO
Balinese Filigree Big Bead

(Top right.) This very large bead was formed in two halves over a wooden ball and then joined by baking. Silver mica powder has transformed the extruded black clay, and a doubled cord completes an eye-catching pendant. Artist's collection.

PATTY SMITH
Black-and-White Beads

(Bottom left.) Thin slices of triangular canes have been applied to create simple but richly textured beads. Using a ball stylus, decoration has been added by pressing contrasting clay dots into dimples on the unbaked beads. The largest bead shown here is 1" (25 mm) in diameter. Artist's collection.

MARGARET REGAN
Bramble Necklace

(Bottom right.) This multi-strand necklace includes a variety of bead shapes illustrating caning and inlay techniques (see pages 30 and 56). The mix of patterns could have been overpowering were it not for the well-chosen spacer beads. Artist's collection.

KAREN LEWIS ("KLEW")
"Drum Circle" Beads

(Top left.) Klew decorated these fabulous beads with slices of different millefiori precision canes, used here in a disciplined format as they are all the same shape and size. The beads were patinated with paint to further enhance their appearance.
Artist's collection.

JANA ROBERTS BENZON
Ball Bracelet

(Top right.) The detail in these beads came from extremely large millefiori precision canes, reduced to form kaleidescope canes, then reduced again. Slices of these cover the bead cores, and the ends are finished with sterling silver end caps.
Artist's collection.

LAYL MCDILL OF SILLY MILLIES
"Wizard of Oz" Bracelet

(Bottom left.) This bracelet uses picture canes with characters from *The Wizard of Oz*. The wonky bead shapes and incongruous sparkling red shoe bead all add to the humor of the piece. Are those pea-green spacer beads cabbages?
Artist's collection.

MARGARET REGAN
Queen of the Nile Necklace

(Bottom right.) A dazzling use of an ordered spectrum of tube beads, embellished with gold foil highlights, creates this wonderful necklace. The strands are spaced with black beads and kept in line with separator bars at each end.
Artist's collection.

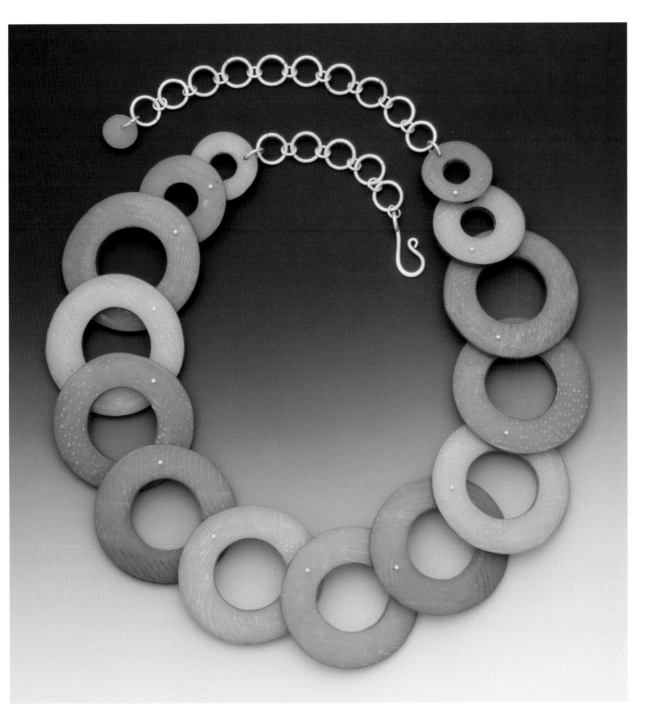

LOUISE FISCHER COZZI
Wholey Necklace
An elegant necklace of overlapping disk beads cut to shape with cookie cutters, and connected with silver rivets. The translucent clay is colored with oil paints that were infused in the clay before baking. Note how the chain can be adjusted and complements the disk beads—a beautifully resolved design. Artist's collection.

MARGARET REGAN
Red Raven Necklace
The artist has developed a special technique for reducing an irregular cane to create a defined shape, in this case a raven, which has been inlaid (see page 56) into rounded red beads with a swirly grain pattern. Note how the screw clasp fastener forms a complete bead when closed.
Artist's collection.

SYNDEE HOLT
Threaded Beads

(Top left.) This interesting bead shape has been created by taking a mica clay cane, cutting it in half, rejoining it, and then marking it into segments. Its constructed form contrasts well with the more natural shapes of the stone spacer beads. Artist's collection.

ALISON GALLANT
Necklace

(Top right.) This necklace of sliced and folded bead shapes was made from a Skinner blend jelly roll (see page 34) of maroon and gold mica polymer clay. The "beehive" beads exploit the shimmering appearance of mica clay. Maroon spacer beads add definition to the necklace.
Author's collection.

JANET PITCHER AND KELLY STEINDORF/ TWOCAN CLAY
Plentiful Produce Necklace

(Bottom left.) These colorful fruit beads were made using the millefiori cane method. The thread holes were drilled after baking, and the beads were threaded with glass and metal spacer beads. Artist's collection.

SUSAN BERKOWITZ
Purple Hearts Necklace

(Bottom right.) A mass of small beads made from polymer clay, glass, and metal have been woven around larger hollow heart beads made of tinted translucent polymer clay. The largest is 2" (50 mm) in diameter.
Artist's collection

TRACY VAN BUSKIRK
Faux Ivory Pendant

(Top left.) This sensitively executed faux ivory bead has been scored and textured to mimic the appearance of antique ivory (see page 74). The crack lines and button decoration were patinated and polished to create a much-handled effect. Artist's collection.

TRACY VAN BUSKIRK
Millefiori Flower Pendant

(Top right.) This bead has been richly decorated with slices of millefiori precision canes rolled into the surface as an inlay (see page 56). The bead is mounted on a head pin with silver end caps and a hanging ring bead. Artist's collection.

LYNNE ANN SCHWARZENBERG
Wind Chimes Bottle Pendant Necklace

(Bottom left.) This bead and pendant combination share a chrysanthemum-style cane. The extruded clay end caps and molded decoration on the bottle add texture. Artist's collection.

LYNNE ANN SCHWARZENBERG
"Paradise Island" Bead Pendant

(Bottom right.) This large lentil bead is composed of translucent and pearl clay with layered foils and other colors swirled in to form a background. Millefiori cane slices form a scene topped by a floating butterfly, also made from a cane. Artist's collection.

DAN CORMIER
Nine Bead Necklace

(Left.) These elegant beads—the largest is 1½ " (38 mm) long—are built from mica and subtly colored stacks of polymer clay. The step-blended stacks were cut and repositioned to form simple grid patterns —a technique also used by makers of patchwork quilts. Decorative veneers were then sliced from the stacks with a sharp peeler. The articulated silver cord complements perfectly the cool precision of the asymmetrically composed beads. Author's collection.

CITY ZEN CANE
Necklace

(Right.) This necklace is a vintage collector's piece from the late 1980s made by City Zen Cane's Steven Ford and David Forlano (now known as Ford/Forlano). This treasured necklace achieves its gradations and shadings by stepped mixes of black and white—a pre-Skinner blend technique. The beads represent a rich mix of canes such as jelly roll, bull's eye, and lace canes (see pages 28 and 30), as well as striped veneers. Note the "CZC" signature cane.
Dana Goodburn Brown Collection.

DONNA KATO
Necklace

(Top left.) This bold necklace contains a mix of paired and dissimilar beads. The round and bun shapes are decorated in a variety of appliquéd jelly roll and bull's eye canes. The decorated thread holes of some beads suggest brightly colored interiors.
Artist's collection.

GAIL WOODS
Patterned Cube Bead Necklace

(Top right.) These cube beads were covered with patterned clay veneers; an ideal use for decorative clay sheets left over from other projects. The polymer clay ring in the center forms part of a toggle fastener.
Author's collection.

ALISON INGHAM
Swirl Lentil Bead Bracelet

(Bottom left.) The tiny swirls on these delicate beads were made by placing two decorative cane slices on each side of a clay ball (see page 27). The copper wirework and the brass swivels complement the delicate swirls in the beads.
Artist's collection.

DONNA KATO
Squiggle Bead Necklace

(Bottom right.) These beads were made from a slice of a layered stack of Skinner blended clays (see page 22). The beads have then been threaded on to rubber cord. The quirky shapes and pastel colors give a light, summery feel.
Author's collection.

Author acknowledgments:

Thanks to all the generous polymer clay artists who have shared their knowledge through their publications, websites, at classes, and at guild meetings. In North America these include Donna Kato, Lisa Pavelka, and all at the San Diego Polymer Clay Guild, especially Jami Miller and Ellie Hitchcock. In Great Britain, Alison Gallant and Alison Ingham of the British Polymer Clay Guild fired my interest in polymer clay, and Sue Heaser encouraged me to write the book. Many thanks to all the people involved in producing this book including editor Liz Dalby.

I tested the patience of photographer Paul Forrester and relied on the expertise of art director Moira Clinch; together we had a lot of fun during the photo shoots and became good friends.

To all the people who lent work for the gallery, thank you.

And most of all, thanks to Derek.

Useful links:

British Polymer Clay Guild www.bpcg.org.uk
Glass Attic www.glassattic.com
Polymer Clay Central www.polymerclaycentral.com
Polymer Clay Daily www.polymerclaydaily.com
San Diego Polymer Clay Guild www.sdpcg.org

Quarto would like to thank the contributing artists for kindly submitting work for inclusion in this book: Donna Kato 105br; Janet Pitcher and Kelly Steindorf 105 (Magnetic clasps); Margaret Regan 104br, 104bl. All other artists are acknowledged beside their work.

Quarto would like to thank the following for supplying materials: Polyform Products Company (www.sculpey.com); Poly-Tools Inc (www.Poly-Tools.com); Ranger (www.rangerink.com); Rupert, Gibbon & Spider, Inc. (www.jacquardproducts.com); Staedtler (UK) Ltd. (www.staedtler.co.uk); syndee holt (www.synspage.com); The Polymer Clay Pit (www.polymerclaypit.co.uk); Tonertex Foils Ltd (www.tonertex.com); Van Aken International (www.vanaken.com).

Quarto would also like to acknowledge the following photographers: Marcia Albert 118tl; syndee holt 117bl, 125tr; George Post 118br, 120; William Sacco 117tr; Hap Sakwa 117br. All other photographs are the copyright of Quarto Publishing plc.

While every effort has been made to credit contributors, Quarto would like to apologize should there have been any omissions or errors—and would be pleased to make the appropriate correction for future editions of the book.